AF207456

THE COLD WAR

1945 – 1991

THE COLD WAR

Michael Kerrigan

amber
BOOKS

First published in 2023

Copyright © 2023 Amber Books Ltd

Published by Amber Books Ltd
United House
London N7 9DP
United Kingdom
www.amberbooks.co.uk
Facebook: amberbooks
Instagram: amberbooksltd
Twitter: @amberbooks
Pinterest: amberbooksltd

ISBN: 978-1-83886-261-9

Editor: Michael Spilling
Designer: Mark Batley
Picture research: Terry Forshaw

Printed in Malaysia

Contents

Introduction

'We will bury you,' the Soviet premier Nikita Khrushchev warned his Western enemies in a speech to the United Nations in November 1956. To this day, it isn't clear whether he meant that the communists would inter the capitalists in the ruins of their cities in a nuclear apocalypse or simply outlast them, thanks to the superiority of their socialist system. But then so it was to live in the shadow of a confrontation that might have more or less destroyed the world in a matter of hours yet which had arguably already kept the peace for several years.

MAD

An entire international order had been constructed on ambiguities of this kind. In Europe especially, communism and capitalism had been facing off for a decade, their restraint compelled by that equilibrium of fear that became known as 'mutually-assured destruction' (aptly abbreviated to 'MAD').

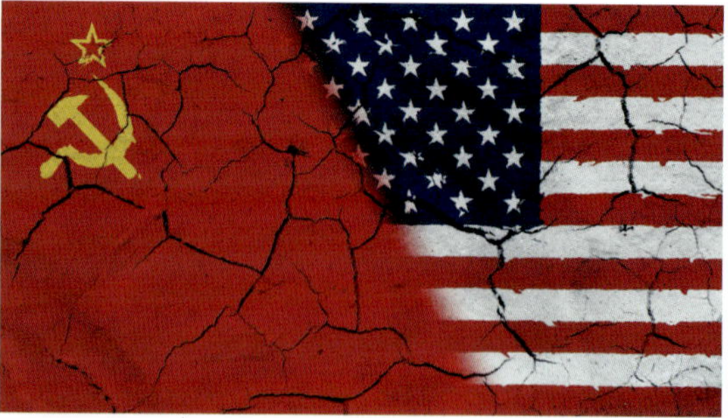

ABOVE:
CLASH OF SYMBOLS
The Soviet flag was a statement – a slogan even – the hammer and sickle standing for the workers in industry and agriculture; the red for the blood they'd shed. The US flag was more mundane in its message, its 13 stripes the founding colonies; the stars the modern states. Their rivalry in the Cold War era represented not just a geopolitical enmity but a wholesale opposition of value systems.

Commentators had struggled for some time to come up with a way of characterizing this sort of conflict. The term 'Cold War' had first been popularized by the English writer George Orwell, and this had stuck. Orwell, though a leftist by his own convictions, was withering in his contempt for the totalitarianism of the USSR. The Union of Soviet Socialist Republics, to give it its full title, was nominally a democracy – a super-sized collective of workers' co-operatives. In reality, he felt, its people were enslaved. America's vaunted 'liberty' might not have meant too much to its downtrodden poor, but there was at least the chance of real representation there.

LEFT:
MUTUALLY ASSURED DESTRUCTION
A *Daily Mirror* cartoon from 1954 shows President Dwight D. Eisenhower and the UK's Winston Churchill trading insults with then Soviet premier Nikolai Bulganin. Superpower conflict, Eisenhower had warned, would mean a world lain waste, 'civilization destroyed' and humankind condemned to start the long and painful evolution out of savagery from scratch.

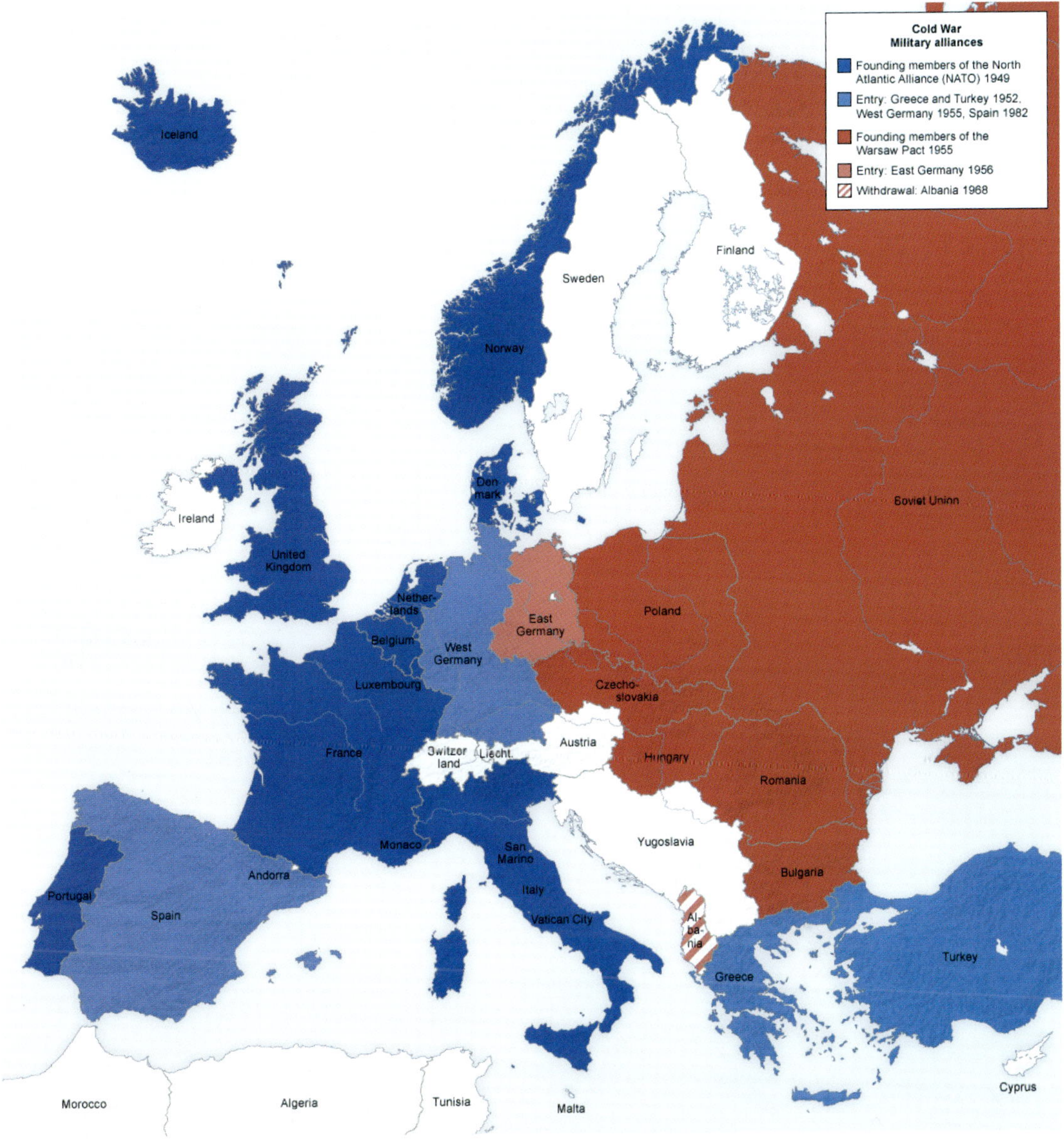

COLD WAR COCKPIT

The Cold War encompassed the whole world but for a half a century its front line was to lie in Europe.

The view of the Cold War as essentially a half-century-long stand-off is of course a hopelessly Eurocentric one. As we will see, the stability that was (mostly) maintained along the 'Iron Curtain' was achieved in large part by the spilling over of conflict into other areas of the world. And, to some extent, by its displacement into alternative spheres – from sport to space exploration; from development assistance to the arts.

It already reads like history but for a whole generation who even now are not quite old, the Cold War confrontation shaped the world.

They learned to live simultaneously threatened and protected by the prospect of nuclear war or endured terrifying, tragic conflicts in countries apparently far removed from the ideological front lines – just so the overall 'balance of power' might be maintained.

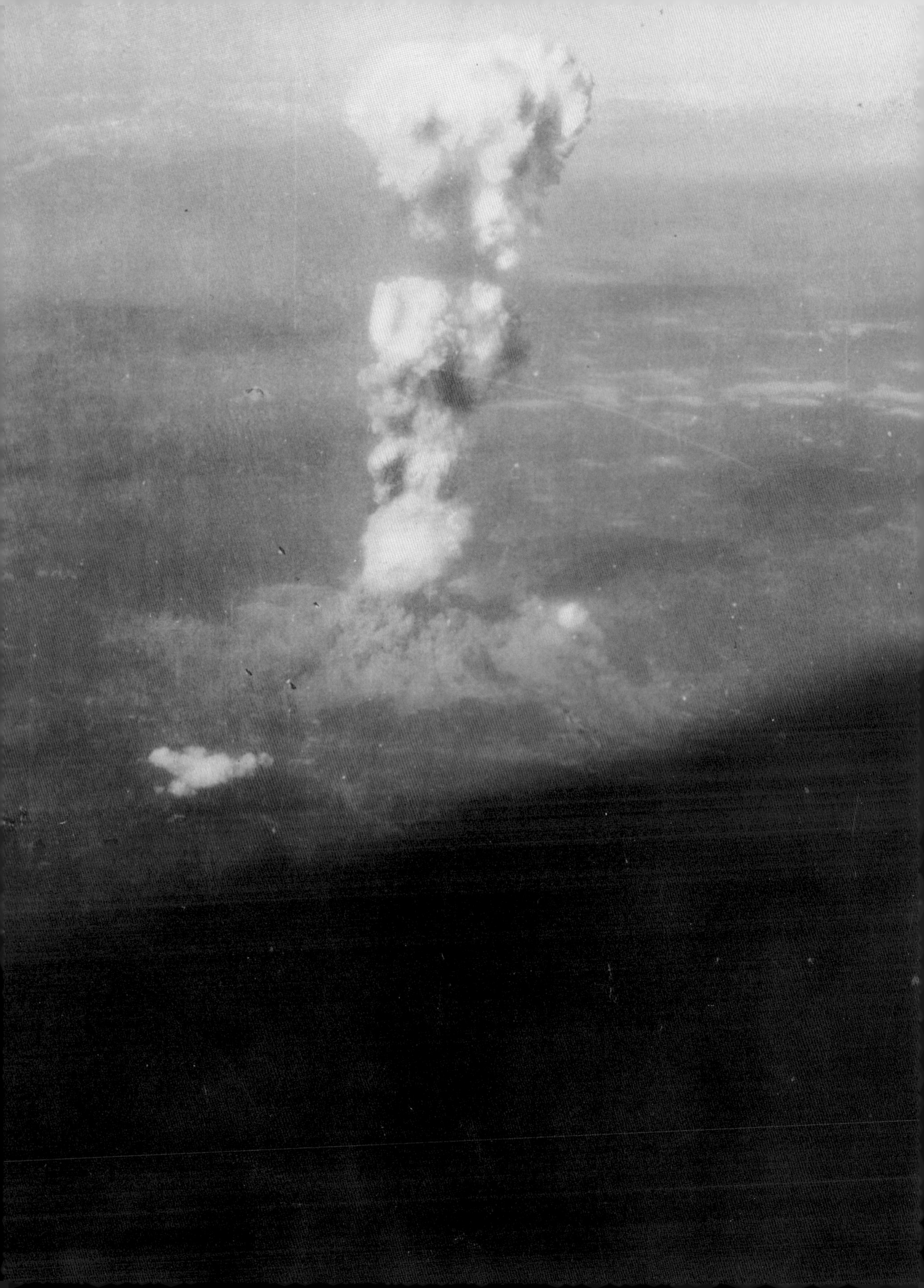

1940s

World War II was barely under way when the 1940s started. Neither the United States nor the Soviet Union was yet involved. In hindsight, we can see how this or that development in the war would have a bearing on the East–West conflict to come, even if it wasn't clear at the time. Stalin's readiness to agree to the Molotov–Ribbentrop Pact with Nazi Germany in August 1939 had underlined his ruthless cynicism in Western eyes; his subsequent annexation of the Baltic States in 1940 made his expansionist aspirations all too clear.

For his part, despite Western protestations of good faith, Stalin suspected that his allies' slowness in opening up a 'Second Front' in southern Europe signalled their willingness to see the USSR all but destroyed before the war was won. Meanwhile, the German V2 rocket arrived on the scene too late to affect the outcome of the war, but in plenty of time to give world leaders pause for thought.

By the end of 1943, however, an Anglo-American army was advancing up through Italy, where the fascist dictator, Benito Mussolini, had been overthrown. By the middle of 1944, Soviet forces had thrown back the German advance in Russia and were pushing forward in their turn, while the Western Allies had taken the initiative in the Pacific.

OPPOSITE:
UP IN SMOKE
The dropping of the first atom bomb over Hiroshima in August 1945 hastened Japan's surrender at the end of World War II. It also served as a warning shot to America's other enemies – a hint at the untold firepower that might yet be unleashed.

OPPOSITE:
REDUCED TO RUBBLE
The great port city of Nagasaki was more or less razed by the blast from the second atomic bomb when it was dropped on 9 August 1945. Here, we see the Roman Catholic cathedral, an instant ruin.

LEFT:
GATEWAY TO NOWHERE
The Sanno Shrine – a Shinto temple – stood only 800 m (875 yards) from the explosion's epicentre and was for the most part levelled to the ground. This gateway's arched construction allowed the blast to go through and round, so this particular structure survived unscathed.

BELOW:
ATOMIC ANNIHILATION
The bomb left Nagasaki a scene of utter devastation. Up to 80,000 people are believed to have been killed.

Until now, it had felt like tempting fate even to imagine a successful conclusion to the conflict; by the start of 1945, it seemed like something that should be planned for. Hence, in February, a conference at Yalta in the Crimea was convened, at which the Allied leaders could discuss the post-war order. The Soviet dictator, Josef Stalin, played host to US President Franklin Delano Roosevelt and Britain's Prime Minister Winston Churchill.

While the defeat of Nazism was a cause for jubilation, it was already becoming clear that liberation was going to mean something very different in Western Europe than in an Eastern Bloc (East Germany, Poland, Czechoslovakia, Bulgaria, Romania, Hungary, Albania and Yugoslavia) under Soviet domination. Yet such had been the sacrifices made by the Soviet Union and its contribution to the defeat of Germany that it hardly seemed this authority over the area could be refused.

Nevertheless, the Yalta Agreement of 1945 left a residue of resentment in the West. Winston Churchill in particular was disgusted at what he saw as a capitulation to tyranny. Though quick off the mark in sensing the danger represented by Hitler and the rise of Nazism in the 1930s, and admirably obstinate in denouncing it at a time when many in his own country weren't really ready to listen, he'd been an outspoken and vehement opponent of the Soviet Union since its foundation in 1917.

RIGHT:
'FRENEMIES'
The 'Big Three' (from left to right: Stalin, Roosevelt and a slightly sulky-looking Churchill) put on a show of calm determination and solidarity at Yalta. Behind the scenes, relations were more wary.

RESIDENT OF THE UNITE

(He would several times subsequently express the regret that the Bolshevik 'baby' had not been 'strangled in its cradle').

The defeat of Hitler in May 1945, welcome as it was, left the war only half-won as far as he was concerned. He certainly saw no reason for the Western democracies to rest on their laurels. Indeed, a few weeks later, in June, when the dust had yet to settle, he tried to persuade President Truman to sign up to an immediate Anglo-American invasion of a war-weakened USSR. (Harry S. Truman had been vice-president to Roosevelt, and succeeded him when he died suddenly that April on the eve of victory). Churchill gave his plan the melodramatic code name Operation *Unthinkable*.

'UNTHINKABLE'

And unthinkable it was, as far as Truman was concerned. Almost as unthinkable for us now is Churchill's easy assumption that he could chivvy, push and even patronize a US president. It didn't seem quite so presumptuous, though, at the time. Britain, after all, ruled over a vast and wealthy empire; though dominant in its hemisphere, America was still an emergent power.

In 1945, however, history was in fast-forward. Just a few weeks later, the global order changed. Its moral order, too, some said. On 6 August, 'Little Boy', the first atomic bomb, was dropped on the Japanese city of Hiroshima by a B-29 Superfortress, the *Enola Gay*. It destroyed the city completely at the cost of over 70,000 lives (tens of thousands more dying from the effects of radiation in the longer term).

Defenders of the American action point to the enormous numbers of lives it saved by cutting short the Pacific War, which was brought to a close after the dropping of a second bomb on the port city of Nagasaki three days later.

Stalin was in no doubt that, whatever the devastation wrought on Hiroshima and Nagasaki, he had been a 'target' of these attacks as well. He was surely right that they'd been a warning of worse to come for the Soviet Union, if he should overstep the mark – though there had been a message in them for Churchill and other leaders, too.

OPPOSITE ABOVE:
CURTAIN CALL
At Westminster College, Fulton, Missouri, Churchill speaks of an 'Iron Curtain' extending all the way down 'from Stettin in the Baltic to Trieste in the Adriatic'. While he doesn't seem to have coined the phrase, he certainly popularized it: it became the classic formulation of the divisions that the Cold War brought.

OPPOSITE BELOW:
TITO
Josip Broz, or Marshal Tito, had led the Yugoslav partisans in their heroic resistance against the Germans during the war. However, though a loyal communist, he would subsequently prove just as resistant to Stalin's bullying, leading Yugoslavia out of the Soviet Bloc in 1948.

OVERLEAF:
STEPPING FORWARD
Soviet-inspired insurgents were more than happy to fill the gap left by the withdrawal of defeated Japanese forces in Eastern Asia. Here, we see soldiers of the Vietnamese Viet Minh in what before the war had been the French colonial territory of Indochina.

ATOMIC ATOLL
In the 1940s and '50s, the
Bikini Atoll, a sometime Pacific
paradise in the Marshall
Islands, became the main
testing site for the US atomic-
weapons programme. Its entire
population was removed by
force and relocated, so that
testing and development could
proceed unchecked.

A war of rhetoric began, Stalin waxing eloquent on the incompatibility of communism and capitalism – conflict between them was 'inevitable', he warned a meeting of Moscow voters in February 1946. A few weeks later, Churchill fired off an answering salvo from Fulton, Missouri: an 'Iron Curtain' had descended over Europe, he declaimed.

LIBERATION STRUGGLES

The effects were experienced along the European front line and far beyond. In 1946, civil war broke out in newly liberated Greece. Leftist partisans were backed by the Soviet Union while Winston Churchill sent assistance to monarchist fighters, who won support as well. No one seriously believed that either of these Western powers cared about King George II of Greece. They were worried that Soviet influence was spreading across southeastern Europe and western Asia. This preoccupation, and America's determination to address it, saw the 'Truman Doctrine' being asserted the following year. The US president promised governments US support against communist insurgencies in Greece and Turkey.

A template was quickly established by which the USSR showed itself ready to endorse left-wing 'liberation struggles'; the US to lend support to those who fought back in the name of 'freedom'. That a little 'liberation' might not have gone amiss in the Soviet Union – a one-party state, rigid and repressive – would scarcely matter, any more than the fact that America's champions of 'freedom' would tend to be right-wing tyrants.

In the first years of the war, a rampantly expansionist Japan had helped itself to European territorial possessions across the East. From British Burma to the Dutch East Indies and from French Indochina to the US-run Philippines, colonial administrations were swept aside. The withdrawal of Japan's defeated forces left a vacuum that the exhausted European nations weren't really in a position to fill. Soviet-inspired insurgents were more than happy to take advantage.

Not that they had things all their own way. France, for instance, fought tooth and nail to hold on to its old colony in Indochina (roughly, Vietnam, Cambodia and Laos). In 1946, in the immediate aftermath of the Japanese departure, the communist Ho Chi Minh and his Viet Minh guerrillas had seized power. Under Soviet sponsorship, they set up the so-called Democratic Republic of Vietnam. However, the French had sent out an expeditionary force, with British help, to take the country back.

The French–Indochina War was to drag on for years until the French were finally defeated at Dien Bien Phu in May 1954. Even then, the situation wouldn't really be resolved.

OPPOSITE ABOVE:
WAR BY PROXY
Guerrilla groups like this one fought a heroic struggle for what they saw as people's rule in Greece; anti-communists battled as bravely for their vision of their country's freedom. What neither side yet saw was that they were pawns in what was becoming a global game of chess between the superpowers.

OPPOSITE BELOW:
PEOPLE POWER?
Men and women fought side by side in left-wing groups like the National Liberation Front and the Greek People's Liberation Army, idealists ready to sacrifice everything for their cause. However, ordinary 'people' couldn't possibly appreciate the extent to which their struggles were simply subplots in a grander narrative of Cold War opposition.

COLONIAL TWILIGHT
Toulon, France, January 1947.
French soldiers prepare to
embark on the *Ile de France* for
service in Indochina. But just
why should their patriotic duty
take them to the other side of
the world, to someone else's
country? For the Allied side,
World War II had been that
comparatively rare thing, a fight
for right, demonstrably just.
Now the international picture
looked different, more complex.

YOU ARE NOW ENTERIN

While Ho Chi Minh had his communist country in the north of Vietnam, a succession of US-backed dictatorships held sway in the south, in the 'Republic of Vietnam'.

IDEOLOGICAL DIVIDE

In Europe, meanwhile, the ideological opposition between communist East and capitalist West was quickly hardening. No longer just rhetorical, it was having an impact on the ground. Churchill's fears that the Yalta Agreement represented 'one of the most melancholy moments in the continent's history' were being borne out by the month as Stalin stamped his authority within his sphere.

Naturally enough, perhaps, Germany was taken under direct rule by the victorious Allies. Stalin set up a Soviet-style communist state in 'his' eastern section. Elsewhere in Eastern Europe, some pretence at maintaining democracy – or at least the autonomy of individual nations – was maintained, though the political wind was blowing one way only.

In Albania, Enver Hoxha's communist partisans had been in control since the final months of the war. As in Greece, leftist groups had earned a certain moral authority. In every country the Germans had conquered there had been widespread active collaboration and passive acquiescence. This response may have been less than heroic, but it was human.

LEFT:
FREEDOM FRONTIER
On one side, capitalist exploitation; on the other, communist repression. Each side claimed a monopoly on 'freedom'. The 'Iron Curtain' wasn't a literal thing, but it had real implications for real lives – and in Central Europe at any rate it was a real frontier. Here, we see the entrance to the American sector in post-war Austria.

Between their ideological convictions and their understanding that, with their known views, they could expect no mercy from the Nazis, communist activists had seen no possibility of accommodation with the occupiers. Naturally, then, they had been in the forefront of the resistance.

The same pattern was to some extent to be replicated elsewhere in Eastern Europe. Socialism wasn't entirely imposed by force. In Bulgaria, for instance, a popular vote in 1946 brought the abolition of the monarchy and the democratic election of a communist government. That this government, once installed, set about co-opting or suppressing all the other parties is the story's less inspiring side.

DEMOCRACY UNDER DURESS

Something of the same happened in Romania, where a communist-led coalition was elected, only for the communists' coalition partners to be quietly removed. In Hungary, the opposition parties won at the polls – only for the communists to seize power in a coup and establish repressive rule. Stalin was for the most part happy to sit out the squalid politicking, waiting to welcome his new allies once they'd taken their 'democratic' decision to join the fold.

But he wasn't going to leave it all to chance. When, in 1947, with Polish polls approaching, the opposition looked like winning, the Soviet dictator invited their leading politicians to Moscow for talks. They were never heard from again; their parties promptly collapsed, and the communists swept to power in Poland.

Czechoslovakia fell in 1948. Only communists could stand in that year's elections. Not surprisingly, the communists were voted in. That same year, in a rare reverse for the USSR, Marshal Tito stood up to Stalin and led Yugoslavia out of the Soviet sphere: his country would remain communist, but would follow its own pathway, he announced.

BUYING ALLEGIANCE?

Meanwhile, April 1948 had seen the inauguration of the Marshall Plan. This was named for the US Secretary of State George C. Marshall, who had drawn it up. He felt strongly that if America took practical and generous steps to rebuild the war-ravaged European economy it would also build enduring peace – and its own prestige. The Western European nations needed no persuading: the United Kingdom was the greatest beneficiary, but France, West Germany and other countries also received support.

In an apparent excess of magnanimity, America offered this assistance not just to Western Europe but also to the USSR and the Iron Curtain countries. The Soviets refused, as (under a certain amount of pressure) did the other socialist states. Stalin took the view that the United States was engaged in economic empire-building. He wasn't completely wrong about that, of course.

That said, the decision only underlined the difference that already existed between a Western Europe whose economies, though badly battered by the war, were undergoing rapid reconstruction, and a devastated Eastern Europe, where dereliction reigned.

SMILES AND STEEL
All is cheer in Harry S. Truman's Oval Office. America's 33rd president followed his former boss Franklin D. Roosevelt in feeling that his country should extend its authority and influence around the world in a spirit of generosity. But he also took the toughest of lines on Soviet expansionism, building US defence capabilities and founding NATO.

PRAGUE WINTER
Crowds assemble in Wenceslaus Square on 25 February 1948 in response to the announcement by communist leader Klement Gottwald that the Party has taken power after a coup. The Communist Party had performed creditably in elections two years earlier but their proposals for collectivization had alienated the countryside while urban workers feared wage caps and restrictions on civic freedoms.

LEKÁRNA

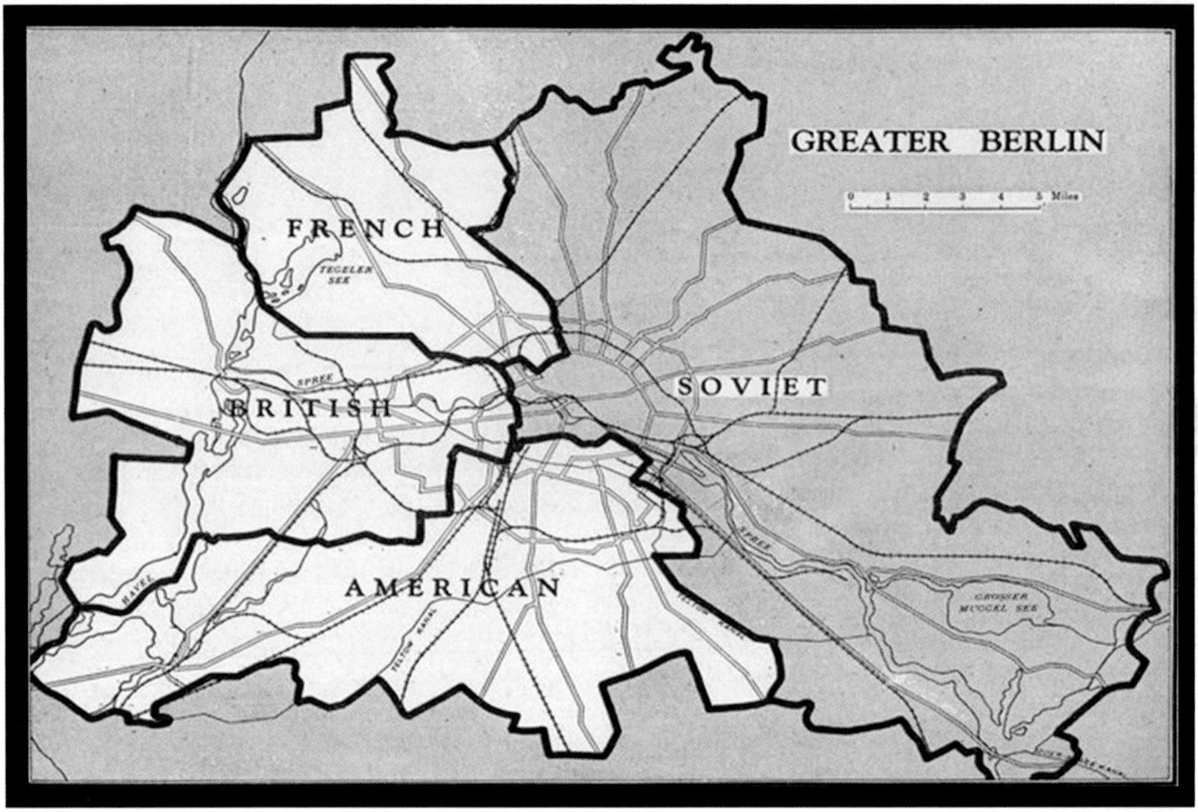

ABOVE:

BERLIN BLOCKADE

On the map, the Soviet sector of Berlin was roughly equal to that of the three Western powers. But the city lay more than 150 km (90 miles) inside the Soviet-controlled DDR. An isolated exclave, 'West Berlin' was reliant on road and rail through communist territory. During the blockade, these corridors were cut off.

RIGHT:

UNDER SIEGE

Through the long months of the Berlin Blockade, the city's people did all they could to secure self-sufficiency. Here, the central strip of the Berliner Strasse has been turned into an allotment for growing fruit and vegetables – even tobacco.

OPPOSITE:

PLANE SPOTTING

However worrying it was for their parents, the Berlin Blockade was an exciting time for boys, who loved to watch the planes taking off and landing.

BERLINER·NOT·PROGRAMM
MIT
MARSHALL·PLAN·HILFE
stapi

Already, the Iron Curtain had ceased to be solely a political and diplomatic barrier: it was now a seemingly impassible economic one.

There had been a sort of soft consensus among the powers that, after a decent interval and with careful safeguarding, East and West Germany would be reunited, as a neutral state. The Soviet Union favoured this outcome because it believed it would be able to discreetly dominate this new Germany; America was doubtful for this same reason. So it was with US encouragement that, in the spring of 1948, the West German authorities came up with plans to introduce a new currency, the Deutsche Mark, which threatened to set such differences in stone.

MARSHALLING RESOURCES
'Emergency Programme Berlin, with the assistance of the Marshall Plan,' the poster reads. US aid was enabling West Berliners to rebuild their city. Over time, it was to become a bustling and successful centre, a high-tech steel-and-concrete reproach to a rather drab and even sleepy East Berlin.

REVOLUTION RENEWED
Shanghai celebrates the proclamation of the People's Republic of China (PRC), October 1949. The long years of civil war are at an end. Though relations between the PRC and the USSR were never entirely easy, this was a clear victory for communism – and a headache for the West.

The communist authorities were enraged. On 24 June, they cut off the roads, railways and canals connecting West Berlin with the Federal Republic: its air links apart, the city was marooned.

Such an outrageously excessive action demanded a quixotically excessive reaction. Western governments organized a massive airlift to keep West Berlin supplied. In the 15 months of the airlift, over a quarter of a million flights (278,228) carried more than 2.3 million tonnes of cargo – food, machine parts, paper, even (enormous amounts of) coal. It was clearly crazy – yet evidently justified, and it did the job.

BREAKING THE BLOCKADE

Initially organized as an emergency measure, the Berlin Airlift quickly proved a propaganda opportunity. The processions of planes flying back and forth made the siege look silly. In no time, indeed, the Berlin Blockade had come to seem an exhibition of slow-witted truculence and intransigence on the communists' part; the Airlift a show of capitalist can-do spirit – an advertisement for Western affluence and abundance. (Some planes dropped showers of sweets for excited children. No tricks were missed …)

Eventually, embarrassed, the East German authorities lifted the restrictions on 12 May 1949 (though, suspicious of an ambush, the British and Americans would carry on flying in supplies for three months more). A few days later, on 23 May, the goal of reunification now clearly off the table, West German parliamentarians drew themselves up a new constitution as the 'Federal Republic of Germany' (FRG). Their East German counterparts had little option but to follow suit a few months later with the establishment of their own Communist 'German Democratic Republic' (GDR). The constitutional division only underscored the economic discrepancy that already existed between the two Germanies by this time.

The West had by now been further buoyed by the signing of the North Atlantic Treaty on 4 April 1949, and the founding of the North Atlantic Treaty Organization (NATO). Any attack on any member would be seen as an attack on all.

COLONIAL CONCERNS

Not that the Western powers had been getting things all their own way during this period. The British Empire was in meltdown in the East. From the middle of 1948, the 'Malayan Emergency' (or, as the rebels saw it, the 'Liberation War') had been raging. If this had been a regular nationalist independence war it would have been worrying enough for London; in the Cold War context, the guerrillas' leftist sympathies made matters worse. In China, the communist leader Mao Zedong was on the brink of victory in his civil war with the nationalists of Chiang Kai-shek. (Many of the Malayan rebels belonged to the Chinese diaspora, in fact.)

By and large, the British at home had little sense of what the colonial life actually entailed. The plantations of Malaya and Singapore were especially idealized. In the popular imagination, droll white gentlemen and elegant white ladies swapped sophisticated witticisms as they sipped gin slings on open verandahs on balmy nights. The wild jungle was just a backcloth, the non-white natives merely obedient foils, setting off the civilization of the scene.

This was a pleasing fantasy, but founded in the most colossal complacency and an utterly unexamined prejudice about the simplicity of the 'native' population and the 'gratitude' they owed.

OPPOSITE:
HUNTING COMMUNISTS
An unknown number of indigenous Dayak tribesmen served with British forces during the Malayan Emergency. Their skills in tracking and their knowledge of the wildest reaches of the forest made them invaluable as guides.

PAIX AU VIET-NAM
NEGOCIER AVEC HO-CHI-MINH
FRANCE VI

MARCHING FOR PEACE
White French and Vietnamese protestors march together through Paris' Place de la Bastille in February 1949 to demand an end to the First Indochina War. Contacts between 'Third World' liberation movements and their own home-grown intellectuals were to become a real bugbear for governments in the West.

MAO MAKES HISTORY

Chairman Mao announces the establishment of the People's Republic of China. This was obviously a historic moment for China, but it was a significant moment in the Cold War, too, complicating East–West relations in all sorts of unforeseen ways and introducing new divisions within the communist bloc itself.

A BOLSHEVIK BOMB

The successful testing of its first atom bomb ('First Lightning') on 29 August 1949 was enormously important for the USSR. After years apparently off the pace in the competition with the capitalists, something like parity looked like it might be restored – in military capability, if not as yet in economic power.

This translated, in the context of an independence war, to an attitude of outraged resentment and a ruthlessly racist willingness to commit atrocities of the cruellest kind, including the rounding-up, relocation and killing of civilians and the wholesale slaughter of their livestock.

SOVIET BOMB

Two events, as the 1940s ended, helped bring parity to the Red side in the Cold War. First, in August 1949, Soviet technicians tested their country's first atomic bomb. Then, on 1 October 1949, the People's Republic of China was proclaimed. Now there was a 'Bamboo Curtain' to go with the Iron one.

1950s

On 1 January 1950, Washington D.C. woke up to springlike sunshine and temperatures 7 °C (12 °F) above the winter norm. But any thought that the geopolitical climate might be easing was promptly banished by the thought of Mao's accession in China and the Soviet Union's new status as a nuclear superpower. However, the Cold War came home with a special chill a few weeks later. In a speech to Republican women in Wheeling, West Virginia on 9 February 1950, Senator Joseph McCarthy denounced the communists he claimed had 'infested' the highest levels of American government in their hundreds, and held up a list he said contained 205 names. In the months and years that followed, at the head of the Tydings Committee (a subcommittee of the Senate Committee on International Relations), McCarthy presided over what amounted to an American Inquisition. Politicians, aides, officials and public figures, including artists and actors, were hauled up to defend themselves (as often as not by denouncing others).

THE GRAND INQUISITOR

Joseph McCarthy personified the 'Red Scare' in post-war America, whipping up a frenzy of paranoia in public life. The suggestion that his persecutory zeal came from his own fear of his homosexuality being uncovered rings true psychologically but remains unproven.

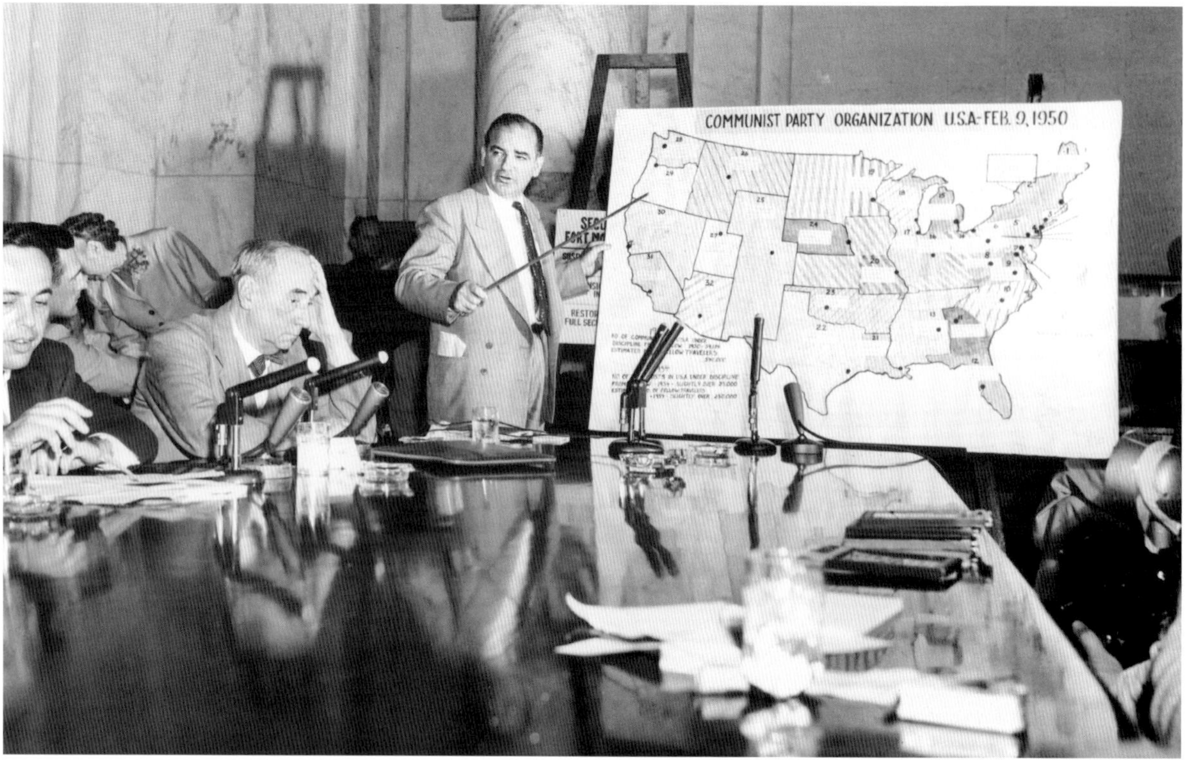
COMMUNIST PARTY ORGANIZATION U.S.A-FEB. 9,1950

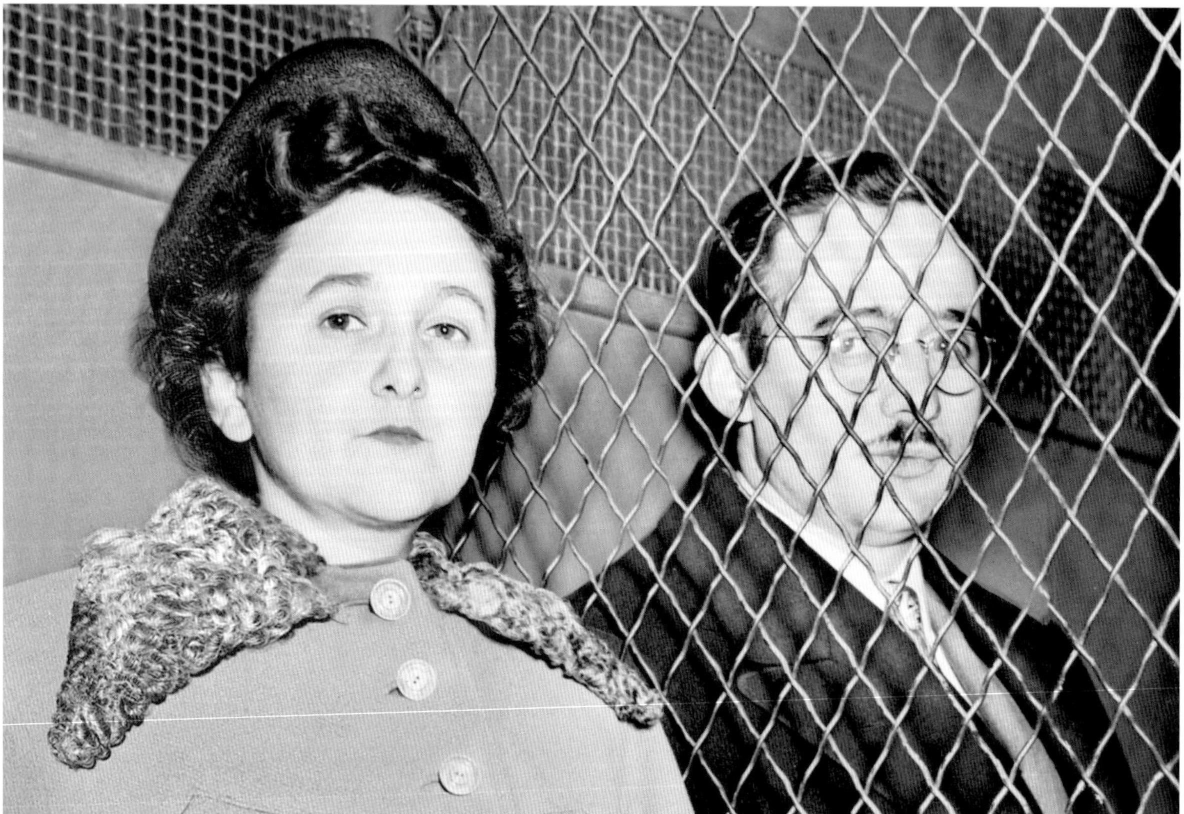

OPPOSITE ABOVE:
THE ENEMY WITHIN
McCarthy maps out the problem, purporting to show the extent of communist activism within the US Army. These televised Senate hearings initially had a powerful public impact but McCarthy's self-promotion proved as tedious as it was tireless and by this time (March 1954), people were already growing weary.

OPPOSITE BELOW:
SOVIET SPIES
Such critics as tried cautiously to suggest that McCarthy was raising exaggerated fears were quelled by the prosecution of Julius and Ethel Rosenberg in 1950. They were subsequently executed in 1953.

LEFT ABOVE:
FRAMED?
Race was always a sticking point in the American national psyche and the McCarthy years were certainly no exception. Even so, TV viewers found themselves unable to see in government clerk Mrs Annie Lee Moss – the picture of respectability and conscientiousness – the Soviet agent McCarthy asked them to.

LEFT BELOW:
SHOW OF FORCE
McCarthy supporters make their presence felt at a rally in Washington D.C., November 1954. Outside the hall, though, the public were beginning to lose interest.

McCarthy seemed vindicated by the arrest of Julius and Ethel Rosenberg in the summer of 1950. That they were New York Jews was in the climate of the time a condemnation in itself, but they faced graver charges. Though both were lifelong members of the Communist Party, Julius had been a government scientist, attached to the atomic weapons programme. With his wife's assistance, he had passed secrets to Soviet contact agents.

'RED SCARE'

Nevertheless, the 'Red Scare' outstripped the Red reality. America was at war with itself. No one could afford to be branded a 'Communist', or even a 'Fellow Traveller', and find themselves unemployable. Groups already seen as having secret lives (like homosexuals) or cosmopolitan loyalties (like Jews) were now viewed as being doubly suspect.

But McCarthy overplayed his hand. People wearied of the incessant outrage and demands for ever-increasing vigilance. Faced with the human reality of its victims and the megalomaniac tendencies they saw in him, Americans lost sympathy with his crusade.

Yet left-wing Americans did exist who – however high-minded their motivation – were ready to help do down the United States and support a Soviet Union which, whether driven by aggression or by fear, wished to shore up its strength at America's expense.

UNITED IN VICTORY
The fifth anniversary of the end of World War II. Some 5,000 German communists, including Prime Minister Otto Grotewohl and his deputy Walter Ulbricht, joined Soviet dignitaries at the war memorial at Treptow, East Berlin, 8 May 1950.

OVER THE TOP
US soldiers storm ashore at Incheon, on Korea's western coast, 15 September 1950. A daring (some had said reckless) amphibious attack, at a time when the invading Korean People's Army had been carrying all before it, its success would help to open the way to Seoul.

Since 1945, it had consolidated its hold in Eastern Europe, effectively establishing an empire there. And, following a pattern set in countries from Greece to Vietnam, it was embarking on a succession of 'proxy wars'.

At the conclusion of World War II, Korea had been divided into a communist North (the Democratic People's Republic of Korea) and a capitalist-supported South (the Republic of Korea). North Korea's Kim-Il Sung, though an avowed communist, was largely driven by his desire for absolute power. His southern counterpart, Syngman Rhee, a proponent of the 'American Way', was concerned with keeping his country safe from corruption. Yet both leaders were loyal to their Cold War backers; and neither accepted the legitimacy of the border at the 38th parallel (latitude 38° north).

Kim it was, though, who on 25 June 1950 sent his Korean People's Army (KPA) across this frontier, catching southern forces napping. Within three days, his force had taken Seoul. It really wasn't difficult. The Americans had been caught napping, too. The distrust they felt for their crooked client had made them wary of supplying much military aid, and they hadn't yet caught on to Moscow's strategic plan.

DELAYED REACTION

They saw it now, and acted quickly, pouring in aid and men with backing from Britain and other allies. The limitations of the KPA and the long supply lines it had left itself with began to tell after America's daring and decisive amphibious assault at Incheon in September 1950. US forces advanced rapidly, General Douglas MacArthur on his own initiative leading them across the 38th parallel into the North. Outrageously overstepping now, he mounted an incursion into Manchuria, bringing an enraged China into the war. The People's Liberation Army sent US forces fleeing south again, while MacArthur mused aloud about the need to use the atom bomb.

Commander of US Army Forces in the Far East during World War II, MacArthur had accepted the Emperor's surrender in Tokyo. A public – and self-consciously heroic – figure, he was known to have political ambitions as a possible presidential candidate for the Republicans and it was against this background that his all-but-mutinous conduct in Korea was inevitably viewed. President Truman was naturally horrified. So too were America's NATO allies, who felt they'd been bounced into something much bigger and riskier than they had signed up for.

Truman unceremoniously sacked his commander. His replacement, General Matthew Ridgway, waged a more cautious war. Many thousands were still to die on both sides, but the struggle eventually subsided until a truce was called on 27 July 1953, leaving the border exactly where it had been before.

OPPOSITE:

TIME OUT

The crew of a US Army M24 tank, members of the 24th Reconnaissance Division, take a breather between bouts of fighting on the Nakdong River front. Fought August–September 1950, the action here was part of the wider Battle of Pusan Perimeter at which American forces saw off an advancing North Korean army.

STRATEGIC WITHDRAWAL
China's intervention in Korea changed the conflict beyond recognition. Rampant just days before, American forces had to about-turn abruptly and head south in haste. The war went on for another two years, its conclusion a modest victory for the West, which had repulsed North Korea's invasion – and learned a lesson about Soviet ambitions in the world.

YOU ARE NOW CROSSING
38TH
PARALLEL
US COB 728MP

Its various proxy wars were instilling the understanding in America's leaders that reaching out to 'my enemy's enemy' was going to involve them making some decidedly dodgy friends. One of these was the Spanish dictator, Francisco Franco. Having first plunged his country into a bloody civil war (1936–9), which he'd won with the help of Hitler and Mussolini, Franco had confirmed himself in power with a campaign of cruel repression. He had remained neutral during World War II itself. Now, a living anachronism after the supposed defeat of far-right rule in Europe, he reigned over what was, near as makes no difference, a fascist state. Whatever he was, though, it had to be admitted that General Franco was no communist. Despite considerable reluctance, President Truman was prevailed on to make overtures to Franco's Spain, even lifting the prohibition that had been previously made on the country's being included in the Marshall Plan.

THE APOSTLE'S CREED

Idealism, however misguided, seems to have driven American traitors like the Rosenbergs; irony appears to have driven their equivalents in England. A group of clever Cambridge students – members of a mysterious (if not quite secret) intellectual society called the Apostles – had adopted communism as their creed in the 1930s.

In fairness, the decade of the Great Depression had been one of desperate hardship for the working class in England as elsewhere, the capitalist system seemingly on the verge of breaking down. So, an interest in the idea of revolutionary change wasn't self-evidently perverse. But there's little doubt that members like Guy Burgess,

Donald Maclean, Harold 'Kim' Philby and Anthony Blunt saw themselves as special, their political extremism marking them out as somehow intriguingly aberrant. Rather as the homosexuality of Burgess and Blunt, and the womanizing of Philby did, it proclaimed their unconventionality to the world.

Communism appealed to them as a sort of super-exclusive club – one they maintained their membership of even now, in the 1950s, despite serving in the highest echelons of the British intelligence service. Donald Maclean was head of the American section in the UK Foreign Office when, in 1951, his treason was uncovered and he was forced to flee to the USSR. Guy Burgess, a diplomat in Washington, went with him, though not yet compromised himself. Kim Philby was to follow them in 1963. (Anthony Blunt was to remain in England, pursuing a distinguished career as an art historian, eventually being placed in charge of the Queen's paintings. He wasn't finally to be unmasked till 1983.)

Meanwhile, Cold War life went on. Britain became a nuclear power, successfully testing an atom bomb on 3 October 1952 in Main Bay, Trimouille Island, in the Montebello Islands in Western Australia. It was playing catch-up, though, for only a few weeks later the Americans tested the first H- (for Hydrogen) bomb: the UK was going to have to get used to playing second fiddle.

HIDDEN IN PLAIN SIGHT
The son of a Liberal MP, and consequently a son of the Establishment and so above suspicion, Donald Maclean had made no secret of his sympathy for communism at Cambridge. A brilliant student, he progressed effortlessly to a place in the Foreign Office and rose in the diplomatic service, reporting to his Moscow handlers all the while.

FLAMBOYANT FRIENDS
English society in the post-war period is seen as having been austere, economically and culturally. And it was; but it had a soft spot for eccentrics. Though still illegal, homosexuality was widely accepted among the elite social circle to which Guy Burgess (left) and his friend, the outrageously 'colourful' left-wing Labour MP, Tom Driberg, both belonged.

ГОСТИНИ
„СОВЕТСК

HO CHI MINH
The man who led Vietnam to its freedom was a serious-minded intellectual. In earlier life he had travelled widely as a ship's cook. He had supported his studies by working as a kitchen hand in France and Britain – and even, briefly, the United States – before spending time in the newly founded Soviet Union.

Not that the communists didn't have their problems. In 1953, the government of the East German workers' state had the ignominy of facing a workers' uprising. Its violent suppression was to be satirized with searing sarcasm by the exiled (Marxist) playwright Bertolt Brecht. In such impossible circumstances, there was only one solution, he suggested: the government would have to dissolve the people and elect another.

World War II cast a lengthy shadow. US President Harry S. Truman, who had given the order for the bombings at Hiroshima and Nagasaki, remained in office until 1953. Americans still felt they were in some sense on a wartime footing. This hardly seemed likely to change with the election of Dwight D. Eisenhower – celebrated as Supreme Commander of the Allied Expeditionary Force in Europe, 1943–5.

OIL WARS

However, with new conflicts flaring up in far-flung places, memories of World War II were beginning to dissipate as new geopolitical priorities asserted themselves. In March 1951, for instance, a left-wing government had nationalized the petroleum industry in Iran – much to the outrage of the British government, who had held a majority stake in the Anglo-Persian Oil Company. America could overlook the financial loss to the British but it feared the way that communistic ideas seemed to be taking hold around the world.

In August 1953, accordingly, the Central Intelligence Agency (CIA) lent its support to a British-backed coup. Iran's elected prime minister, Mohammad Mosaddegh, was deposed. His replacement, Mohammad Reza

Pahlavi, had reigned for some years already as the Shah of Iran, but this had been a constitutional – almost ornamental – role. Now he was a dictator, and a markedly repressive one.

OVERTHROWING ÁRBENZ

Making the world safe for democracy, in Woodrow Wilson's words, now apparently involved a recognition that some (smaller, poorer) nations would have to give up their freedoms for the greater good. Guatemala's elected president, Jacobo Árbenz, was an avowed admirer of the United States. He hoped to bring an American-style system to his country and spread these values through Central America as a whole.

But Americans had rights, and Guatemala's biggest employers, the United Fruit Company, found it more profitable to operate in a country whose people didn't. They objected to Árbenz's plan to distribute vast areas of land they had left unproductive to small farmers. They found a receptive ear in Washington, where policy advisers were now ready to see any programme of reform as a step on to a slippery slope that could only lead to Moscow. And so, with CIA support, a group of military men overthrew Árbenz and raised Carlos Castillo Armas to the presidency. Several years of savage repression followed.

PLAYING DOMINOES

In practice, it was becoming clear, almost anything could be justified in the name of anti-communism. In April 1954, Eisenhower proclaimed the theory. Addressing reporters on the ongoing conflict in Indochina, he spoke of a 'falling domino' principle. When you have a row of dominoes set up and tip over the first one, it knocks over the next, which knocks over the one after that, and so on – until all have fallen over. The dominoes here were countries, of course, in a world in which restlessness and revolution were being fomented by the communist superpowers – the USSR and China – and their clients. When one country went communist, it emboldened (if it didn't actively assist) the next. Before we knew it, much of the free world might well have fallen.

AU REVOIR, INDOCHINE

As though to illustrate Eisenhower's argument, a few weeks later, French forces dug in at Dien Bien Phu, northwest of Tonkin in the north of Vietnam, were dislodged after a determined siege by Ho Chi Minh's insurgents. The United States, though not officially involved, had been keeping France's Far East Expeditionary Force supplied, so this was a blow to American pride as well. It was also food for thought, given the likely consequences. Talks in Geneva now ordered a Korea-style division of Vietnam into a Soviet-backed North and a US-backed South (the Republic of Vietnam).

But Vietnam wasn't the only 'domino' in play. Neighbouring Cambodia had nominally been left a constitutional monarchy by the departing French, but King Sihanouk was under pressure from the communist Khmer Rouge. In Laos, too, a postcolonial kingdom had been established, but this was also under communist pressure from the rebel forces of the Pathet Lao.

OPERATION *RANGER*
Awestruck US troops look on as an atomic device is tested at Frenchman Flat, Nevada, 1951. This was one of a series of five devices that were dropped from B-50D bombers to explode in the air above the dried-up lake.

CHEVROLET
AMERICA
458
MALA-54

READY FOR ACTION
Armas' so-called 'Liberation Army' was a rag-tag crew of mercenaries, recruited the length and breadth of Central America. Here, they assemble at Chiquimula, close to the border of Honduras, where they were originally mustered, ready to go off to the front to join the fighting.

ABOVE:
CIVIL DEFENCE
Newark, New Jersey, schoolchildren take refuge underneath their desks in a nuclear-attack drill, February 1952. Such exercises would become a familiar feature of US school life.

RIGHT:
CLOUD OF GLORY
The successful detonation of an atomic bomb over the Montebello Islands, Western Australia, on 3 October 1952, secured Britain membership to the still-exclusive nuclear club.

OPPOSITE:
THE 'RED CZAR' SLEEPS
Peaceful at last, the late dictator Stalin left a legacy of trauma to his own country – and a reawakened yearning for freedom in his empire.

DÉJÀ VU
Just eight years after the Red Army rumbled into Berlin to bring an end to World War II, Soviet tanks were seen in action on the city's streets again. This time, they were putting down workers who had rebelled against their puppet government in the uprising of June 1953.

Liberals were to sneer at the near-fanatical faith successive US governments placed in what became known as the 'Domino Theory', but there was no doubt that it seemed to be being borne out here.

DICTATORSHIP DENOUNCED

While America was justifying its support of autocratic governments around the world, the Soviet Union was reeling from the impact of its own. Stalin's death in 1953 had obviously been a liberation in some ways, but the country was still trying to come to terms with the murderous fury he had unleashed. Millions had been killed in his paranoid crackdowns; millions more by the famines his ruthless policies had caused; untold numbers of families undone by mass imprisonments and deportations.

Not that the fundamentals had changed. Totalitarianism still reigned in an anti-democratic USSR. But if Nikita Khrushchev was loyal to the Communist Party, he was not a monster. Seeing

ACTION ACCOMPLISHED
General Vo Nguyen Giap views the battlefield at Dien Bien Phu in the aftermath of his forces' historic victory. The final defeat of the French would only bring a brief respite to Vietnam's defenders, but it was nevertheless a triumph – and a powerful fillip for 'freedom fighters' around the world.

LAST-DITCH DISCUSSION
A group of French officers discuss tactics as outside the Battle of Dien Bien Phu continues: this bitter action was to wear on for over seven weeks. France knew all too well that defeat would spell the end to its colonial rule in the Far East; the Vietnamese attackers that this was their only way to freedom.

FAR RIGHT?
A French soldier watches as an aircraft is shot down at Dien Bien Phu. Cynical as Soviet motives might have been, the 'fraternal' aid they had supplied the Vietnamese rebels with had enabled them to engage the European power on something like equal terms.

the need for some sort of healing, he denounced his predecessor at the 20th Congress of the Soviet Communist Party, on 25 February 1956, condemning 'His Intolerance, His Brutality and His Abuse of Power'.

Fair enough, but as many of Khrushchev's comrades would come to feel, the late dictator had at least kept order in the Eastern Bloc. Khrushchev had started well, responding to West Germany's admission to NATO in 1955 with the establishment of a 'Warsaw Pact'. This knit the Iron Curtain countries into a defensive alliance – which should also have strengthened the authority of the USSR. But June 1956 saw a strike at a locomotive factory in Poznán, Poland, turn into a widespread protest at communist rule. It had to be put down violently by the authorities.

HELP HUNGARY

Still more serious was the uprising in October in Hungary that year. Again, the unrest began with workers dissatisfied at their treatment by a Communist Party that claimed to be ruling in their name. They took over Budapest and large areas beyond. They even set up a government, supplanting the rule of the Party with a Council of Ministers chaired by reformist socialist Imre Nagy.

Under fire himself, Khrushchev had little alternative but to order an immediate invasion. Days of fierce fighting followed, during which the rebels broadcasting from Budapest's main radio station made increasingly desperate pleas to the Western powers to help. Their calls fell on deaf ears. Inevitably, communist rule was reinstated under the Party's loyal first secretary, Janos Kadar.

CANAL CARVE-UP

It would never have been easy for the West to intervene in a Hungary it had formally signed over to the Soviet sphere. That Khrushchev was so clearly beleaguered would have done nothing to diminish their nervousness – the USSR was, after all, a nuclear power. But they had in any case been distracted by major events in Egypt, where another international crisis had been unfolding.

Swept to power by a popular vote of 1952, President Gamal Abdel Nasser had already embarked on an ambitious programme of land reform. Cold-shouldered by the West, he had cosied up to the Soviets, who had sold him arms, prompting Western governments to withdraw offers of aid towards his Aswan Dam project.

In response, at the end of October 1956, Nasser had nationalized the Suez Canal, which was administered by a company owned partly by France and partly by Britain. Though Eisenhower warned against it, Britain and France sent paratroops to the Canal Zone while Israel invaded Egypt over Sinai. Egyptian forces along the Canal banks fled, but scuttled shipping along the waterway, leaving the supposed victors with a useless prize. A setback for the West at large, the episode was calamitous for Britain, whose status as a strictly secondary power had been emphatically underscored.

OPPOSITE:
PRAYING FOR PAYBACK
María Trinidad Cruz – the only woman fighting in Armas' right-wing Guatemalan 'Liberation Army' – offers a prayer beneath the grave of her husband, shot by soldiers of Árbenz. Communism was proudly atheistic, even if its allies weren't necessarily, so the iconography of faith was naturally weaponized against it.

ABOVE:

SHOWING THE WORLD

'We shall defend our freedom and independence to the last drop of our blood.' Gamal Abdel Nasser rallies his forces in a speech to cadets, 18 September 1956. His stand was undoubtedly an inspiration to revolutionary movements around the world. The Suez Crisis cast the West as oppressors of 'small countries' at a time when the Soviet Union was crushing Hungary.

OVERLEAF:

THE GROWN-UPS ARE HERE

A UN troop contingent arrives in Port Said, Egypt, to restore order in the confusion that accompanied the Suez Crisis, 1956. Nasser's dramatic actions over the Canal were put down as reckless showmanship by Western commentators, but they won him admiration in a great many poorer countries

OPPOSITE ABOVE:

BESPOKE BRUISERS

A middle-class mob of vigilantes puts on a show of anti-communist strength on the streets of Tehran in the run-up to the Iranian elections of 1954. They hardly needed to: the poll was very clearly rigged to supply the Shah with the endorsement he was seeking.

OPPOSITE BELOW:

A GENEROUS DESPOT

Much as he'd despised Mosaddegh, the Shah had seen how popular his policies had been with ordinary Iranians. In power himself, he steered a canny course between outright repression and paternalist benevolence. Here, a peasant thanks him for the plot he has been awarded under the government's (tokenistic) 'land reforms'.

MILITARY POLICE

SOCIALIST SACRIFICE
A street scene in Budapest, October 1956. These events were to haunt a guilty West, which was well aware it hadn't helped the Hungarians in their time of need. But it was also to trouble the conscience of an Eastern Bloc whose peoples could see how excruciatingly close their neighbours had come to winning their freedom. And how little trouble their Soviet masters – supposedly the protectors of the working class – had taken even to go through the motions of demonstrating any care for their consent.

RÁKÓCZI
376

THE FRONTIER ABOVE

No one now could seriously question the Soviet Union's superpower status. Not that anyone had any interest in doing that. The Cold War wasn't just an episode, a succession of events: it was a logic, a way of thinking, a frame of mind. If it obviously suited the Soviets to sell themselves to their allies and adherents around the world as a leading military force, it wasn't in the interest of America's rulers to gainsay their claims.

Not until 1961 would President Eisenhower give a name to the 'military–industrial complex', but the thing already existed, that was clear. The Soviet threat might be genuine, but it justified a vast economic and technological effort in the United States as bigger, better battleships, bombers, tanks, submarines and small-arms were designed and built. The threat might be frightening for ordinary Americans, but many tens of thousands of them relied on it for their livelihoods, whether enlisted in the military or employed in supporting industries.

The US economy was coming to depend on the Soviet threat. It wasn't in anybody's interest to talk it down. It could of course be argued that this enormous effort might have been targeted on a more worthy aim, all these talents and resources more fittingly applied. In the real world, though, the Cold War was helping lift America out of its post-war economic doldrums and prompting a technological renaissance of a sort.

HEAVENLY BODY
A Soviet technician works on Sputnik I. The satellite was launched in 1957, to the amazement of the world and the shock of the United States. Communism was a materialist creed. In the absence of religion, it invested all its reverence in science and technology.

It came as a special shock, then, when, in 1957, the USSR launched its first satellite, Sputnik I. The Soviets, smugly magnanimous, made all the right noises about what their achievement meant for humankind. And it was true: it was indeed momentous that man had sent an object into space. But the fact that it had been communist man could not but stick in capitalism's craw.

LEAPING INTO THE ABYSS

With the Soviet Union soaring into space, China was running up to take off, too, in 1958 inaugurating the 'Great Leap Forward'. The mass collectivization of agriculture was imposed in the teeth of opposition from traditionally minded peasants – or 'counter-revolutionaries' as Mao's supporters called them, making their denunciation a focus for public rage. Local activists organized 'struggle sessions', at which recalcitrant peasants were paraded before their communities to be yelled at, humiliated and beaten into confessing all sorts of antisocial activities. Armies of peasants were set to work to help dig irrigation and drainage ditches and to extend the country's network of paved roads. An impressive sight, though the more these men and women worked on infrastructure projects, the less attention they could give their paddy fields. This didn't matter to Mao, for whom the appearance of modernization was more important than the reality. Hence the backyard furnaces that sprang up in every village, into which all sorts of scrap was thrown – to be smelted into useless 'steel'. The Great Leap Forward was in fact a flop – a particularly ugly one given the millions who were to be murdered as dissidents or die in the famines the agrarian disaster caused.

OPPOSITE:

WELCOMING THE FUTURE

Chinese villagers rejoice at the arrival of a fleet of tractors
at the time of the Great Leap Forward. Modernization,
they were promised, would revolutionize their lives.
In practice, collectivization was ill-thought-out and
unresponsive to local needs. Production collapsed, famine
resulted and millions died.

ABOVE:

READY TO RANT

Glowering beside a grim-faced Andrei Gromyko, his
minister for foreign affairs, Nikita Khrushchev, prepares
to speak at the United Nations, 1959. Real as Cold War
tensions were, much of the daily 'mood music' was
made by little triumphs and losses of face: Khrushchev's
tantrum here belonged to the latter category.

CHE TRIUMPHANT
Not yet iconic but already influential, the Argentinean Ernesto 'Che' Guevara was a priceless asset to the Cuban Revolution. Here, we see him standing by a tank at Santa Clara on 1 January 1959, after the rebels' culminating victory over Fulgencio Batista's regime.

CASTRO COMES THROUGH

Communism was faring better in the Caribbean where Fidel Castro's Cuban rebels, under arms since 1953, were gaining ground. Despite the cruelty and corruption of Fulgencio Batista's US-backed regime, ordinary Cubans had been reluctant to rise up. The 'colourful' Castro wasn't just a caricature; he'd also shown dogged determination in his cause, bringing his guerrillas through the long years of living rough in the Sierra Maestra, without obvious prospect of victory. Not until 1959 would the rebels ride in triumph into Havana.

'LAW OR BRIGANDAGE?'

The Soviet Union might be able to send a satellite into space but it struggled to protect its skies from US spy planes. So frustrated did Nikita Khrushchev get that he strayed from the script of his speech to the UN in September 1959 to launch a bitter diatribe against America's lawless ways. In his fury, he got as far as removing his shoe and banging his lectern with it to show the strength of his outrage and contempt. A pity in a way: his official speech was a serious and elegantly expressed avowal of the USSR's support for the winding-up of colonialism in the world.

ROAD OF RESISTANCE

The North Vietnamese Army (NVA) was by now opening up the so-called 'Ho Chi Minh Trail'. A series of scanty pathways, the Trail still allowed provisions and materiel to be carried on foot and by bicycle deep into South Vietnam, where Viet Cong (VC) guerrillas were fighting the forces of Ngo Dinh Diem's US-backed government. For much of its length it ran through Laos, which offered security in the short term but would draw that country into the conflict later.

RIFLE DRILL
A scholarly-looking Fidel Castro – not yet the swashbuckling figure in fatigues he would later present – helps train a rebel recruit in the elementary arts of war. Despite the existence of great poverty and injustice in Cuba, Castro's charisma was essential to the success of the revolution there.

1960s

The New Year hangovers had hardly abated when, on 2 January 1960, John Fitzgerald Kennedy announced his candidacy for the Democratic nomination for the US Presidency. At 43, 'Jack' Kennedy was to be the youngest ever Democratic candidate; his decision to stand sent a signal, first to Washington and then the world.

The era we think of as the 'Sixties' now – the music, the drugs, the hippies, the 'free love' – arguably didn't get underway until the decade was half done. But if the years before that for the most part seemed no more than a dour addendum to the 1950s, the Kennedy charisma lifted the time somehow. Despite a distinguished war record, he didn't seem to 'belong' to that past as both Truman and Eisenhower had. He was a figure full of promise for the future.

True, there was a darker side to John F. Kennedy. His whole campaign was managed by his father, Joseph P. Kennedy Sr., a sometime Nazi-sympathizer with gangland connections. Thus, a shadow was to hang over John F. Kennedy's eventual election, and he himself appeared to have his demons.

OPPOSITE:
FIDEL AND FRIENDS
On first-name terms with the world, 'Fidel' was a new and different kind of communist: young, colourful and fun rather than old and earnest, drab and dour. Here, he holds a press conference in Harlem's Hotel Theresa, prior to addressing the United Nations in New York.

Despite efforts to portray his womanizing as just 'Jack the Lad' exuberance, Washington insiders saw more frantic, even desperate drives. In short, the hope he offered appeared to be qualified by unnamed fear and vague foreboding. An ambiguous hero for an ambivalent decade.

Cuba's leader Fidel Castro was even younger – only 34 when, in September 1960, he came to New York to address the United Nations. 'Fidel' to his friends, he seemed a friend to the whole world, and put a friendly face on what could appear a dour and joyless ideology, and gave a certain swagger to the march of progress.

Like Kennedy, Castro had a darker side. His manner might be matey, but he was no democrat. Not only were there no plans for meaningful elections in Castro's Cuba, but the island's prisons were filling up with men and women who had spoken out of turn. Even allowing for official exaggeration, though, the Cuban literacy campaign had been stunningly successful, while health provision was improving by the month. The mass of the poor in the rest of the Caribbean and the Latin American mainland could only dream of the treatment Cubans were beginning to take for granted. Indeed, poor people in the United States could only dream of it, too.

IDEOLOGICAL DIFFERENCES

Good news of this sort was overdue for a communist world still reeling from the Sino–Soviet split, which had taken place that June. The ostensible reasons for it were drily theoretical. Mao's take on Marxism-Leninism was already unconventional given his desire to adapt it to his country's overwhelmingly agrarian economy. (Marx himself had of course been adamant that true communism could only evolve in an advanced industrial economy, a standard even early-20th-century Russia could hardly be seen as having reached.) Cut through the complex dialectic, though, and the real problem appears to have been that an unrelenting Mao disapproved of Khrushchev's de-Stalinization plans, seeing them as soft, liberal and essentially effete.

Whatever the reasons, though, the split had left the Soviet Union that bit more isolated at a time when it was already feeling vulnerable in certain ways. Khrushchev's angry outburst at the United Nations the previous year had betrayed his agitation at the activities of America's spy planes, which seemed to be able to criss-cross Soviet airspace pretty much at will. That in May 1960 his forces had succeeded in bringing down a U-2 plane with a surface-to-air missile over the Urals and had subsequently captured its pilot, Gary Powers, was on the one hand a coup and on the other a reminder of what was going on. US airmen were apparently all but commuting across the USSR. Though they were happy to be able to arraign Gary Powers, try him and send him to a Russian prison for two years, it was with some relief that they eventually traded him for Soviet KGB Colonel William Fisher, known as 'Rudolf Abel', a Soviet spy.

REVOLUTIONARIES
Staying in Harlem with the poor and dispossessed on his visit to New York in September 1960, Castro was well-placed to receive the leaders of America's emerging civil rights movement. There was mischief in his meeting Malcolm X, for sure – it would obviously embarrass the US government. But his credentials as a fighter against injustice were well established.

FIRST AMONG EQUALS?
Brandishing a clenched fist, Soviet premier Nikita Khrushchev delivers an angry tirade at his farewell press conference in Paris, May 1960. Despite repeated booing from the audience, the Russian leader warned that further American spy flights over the Soviet Union would lead to war. Khrushchev also compared President Eisenhower to 'a thief caught red-handed in his theft'.

THE MAN WHO FELL TO EARTH

Well and truly grounded now, Gary Powers faces his accusers in a Moscow court, 18 August 1960. He could hardly deny the charge of espionage, having been shot down over Russia, hundreds of miles from the nearest border. After a couple of years in prison, he was freed, but faced a frosty welcome on returning to America. Some blamed him for not avoiding capture by taking his suicide pill before he landed; others even suspected him of self-sabotaging with a view to defecting.

THE HAPPY COUPLE
America's president-elect, John F. Kennedy stands on stage at the Hyannis Armory, Massachusetts, to make his acceptance speech, his wife Jacqueline, 'Jackie', at his side. Consciously or not (though very likely the former), his address laid emphasis on their youth and vigour and the possibilities they brought for regeneration. 'So now my wife and I prepare for a new administration and a new baby,' he concluded.

In Africa, meanwhile, the United States was still playing dominoes. Fighting off the forces of France and Belgium, the idealistic Patrice Lumumba had secured independence for the Republic of Congo (now the DRC). 'We're no longer your monkeys,' he informed the European powers. As the Republic's first president, he faced a mutiny of army officers put up to it by the former colonial powers. He had asked America for help but been refused. His decision to turn to the Soviet Union for assistance had sealed his fate. The United States joined France and Belgium in backing a coup by Lumumba's chief-of-staff, Joseph-Désiré Mobutu. Lumumba was captured and summarily executed.

PIG'S EAR

Cuba was to remain a thorn in America's side through the early 1960s. Kennedy was under considerable pressure to recover what had been a popular holiday destination for Americans. Not least, some said, from friends of his father, who had owned casinos there. But America could never have been comfortable with having a communist country so close by. And then of course there was Castro: always keen to cock a snook.

Despite such compelling reasons, Kennedy's handling of the situation was cack-handed – and perhaps half-hearted. In the summer of 1961, he gave only reluctant backing to an exiles' plot to invade the island with a force of mercenaries. Even then, having committed to providing comprehensive air cover for the landing at Playa Girón (also known as the 'Bay of Pigs'), he rowed back at the 11th hour, allowing only limited support. Predictably, perhaps, the whole operation was a fiasco.

THE WINNERS
Cuban militiamen and soldiers pose for pictures in a captured launch of the Bay of Pigs' invaders. The mood is celebratory, despite heavy casualties. Over the years, US hostility towards Cuba was arguably to boost a communist regime that might otherwise have quickly lost much of its appeal.

WALLED IN
Berliners woke up on 13 August 1961 to find East German soldiers
hard at work ripping up road surfaces and raising a barbed wire
barrier between East and West. The GDR had been embarrassed by
the stream of defectors heading into West Berlin, including many
young and talented men and women. In the days that followed,
the first temporary barrier was replaced by the more permanent
concrete construction we see here.

Unbefugten ist das
Betreten verboten

MRBM FIELD LAUNCH SITE
San Cristobal #1
14 OCTOBER 1962
ERECTOR/LAUNCHER EQUIPMENT
TENT AREAS
8 MISSILE TRAILERS
EQUIPMENT

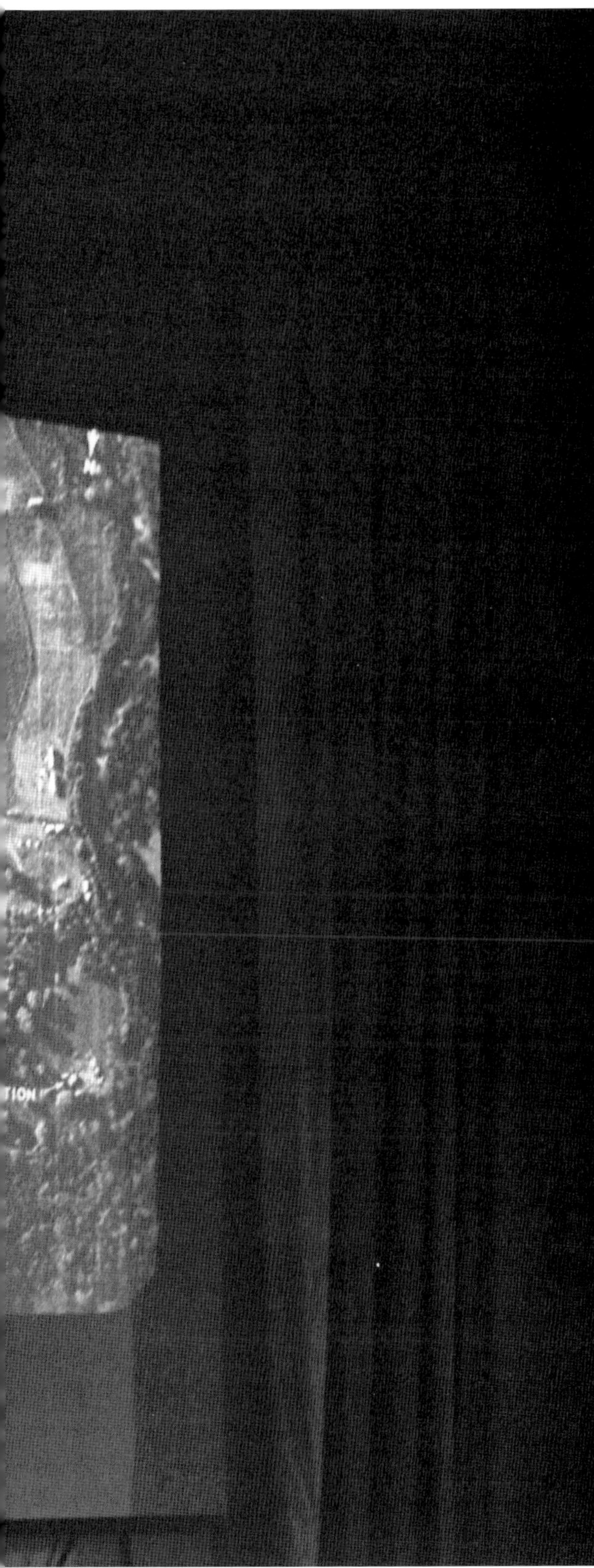

And, conversely, a propaganda triumph for Castro's Cuba. The landing had been expected and the 1,200-strong invasion force was largely captured. Over a hundred were killed in the fighting and hundreds executed afterwards. Cuban losses had been worse – anything up to 2,000 men may have been killed – but the glory was on their side; the ignominy on America's.

That this humiliation came so soon after the USSR had conducted the first manned space flight, sending cosmonaut Yuri Gagarin heavenwards in the Vostok 1 capsule on 12 April 1961, only deepened the resentment on the US side. More positively, though, the event had spurred the United States to action: on 25 May, President Kennedy announced the aim of putting a man on the moon 'before this decade is out'.

SUPERPOWER POKER

The hardening of attitudes was given concrete form that August, when the East German authorities threw up the Berlin Wall. Concerned at the 'brain drain' of its citizens to the West, it built this barrier to keep them in. The people of the Iron Curtain countries were literally prisoners. And hostages, held as it were at gunpoint, given the United States' placing of Jupiter medium-range ballistic missiles at sites in Italy and Turkey over the furious protests of Nikita Khrushchev.

SETTING OUT THE EVIDENCE

A State Department official explains how satellite photos show the construction of a missile base at San Cristóbal, Cuba during the crisis of 1962. It isn't the main point here, obviously, but the quality of this imagery serves to remind us again how Cold War tensions had spurred technological advance.

PRESIDENT
KENNEDY
BE
CAREFUL

PEAC
or
Peris

THE
UN
HANDLE
THE
CUBAN
CRISIS!

WATCHING CLOSELY
Cuban refugees huddle round the TV to watch President Kennedy broadcasting to America about their country's missile crisis. They wouldn't remain spectators for long. Over the years, the Cubans were to engage ever more actively in US politics and make themselves an important electoral force.

WIVES AND MOTHERS
Activists from Women Strike for Peace urge care and caution during the Cuban Missile Crisis, 1962. Over 50,000 women had taken part in protests across the United States the year before. The growing peace movement would be an irritant to successive US administrations.

From the Western point of view, the face of East European communism had always been grim. Now, the Cuban Revolution took a more sinister turn. As long as it had been about free healthcare and happy dance music under the swaying palms of a sunlit paradise, it had been no more than a provocation (if in some ways a reproach as well). Now it appeared it was actually a threat.

On 16 October 1962, photographs taken from a U-2 spy plane over Cuba revealed the construction of facilities for launching intermediate-range nuclear missiles. Castro's government seems to have requested that they be built, concerned to deter further US attacks in the aftermath of the Bay of Pigs invasion, but it clearly suited the Soviet Union's strategic aims as well. Anxious to avoid a shooting war, President Kennedy ordered a naval 'quarantine' of Cuba until the threat to the United States had been removed.

RIGHT:
DREAMER
Dr Martin Luther King Jr., delivers his famous 'I have a dream
…' speech in the shadow of the Lincoln Memorial, the climactic
moment of the March on Washington, 1963. The injustices suffered
by African Americans called into question any claim to moral
authority the West might make. Anger was to grow throughout
the 1960s.

Khrushchev was in no mood to fold. He was
under pressure from his Politburo. His policy of de-
Stalinization had always had its critics among the more
hardline members. His slackness, they hinted, had
been behind the breakdown of socialist order in Poland
and Hungary. He'd been humiliated, too, by the recent
construction of US missile sites in Turkey. Was he really
the man to keep the Revolution safe?

Nor could Kennedy afford to budge. There were
those in the US establishment who felt his blockading
of Cuba had been a limply inadequate response to
outrageous communist aggression. (They hadn't
forgotten his dithering over the Bay of Pigs.)

All-out nuclear war was on the cards. In the West at
least, where press and TV news reported on the crisis
as it unfolded, families went about their lives in real
fear. The Cold War could seem a distant, even abstract
conflict for ordinary people. Now, however, it had come
home with a vengeance.

The stand-off went on for several days. Finally,
though, the Soviets agreed to remove their missiles
in return for an American promise not to mount any
further attacks on Cuba. (More discreetly, they also
undertook to take their own missiles out of Turkey.)
On 20 November, the US naval blockade was lifted.

CAMELOT CURTAILED

On 22 November 1963, America was rocked by
the news that President John F. Kennedy had been
assassinated in Dallas, Texas. The event was attended
by irregularities and surrounded by confusion.
Shooter Lee Harvey Oswald, an ex-marine, had
spent time in the Soviet Union and brought home a
Russian wife; Kennedy had obviously made enemies
in both the USSR and Cuba. Quickly, though, the
speculation started to focus on the Kennedy family's
organized crime connections and the suggestion
that the president was felt to have let his mafia
sponsors down.

Viewed dispassionately, his presidency had
been lacklustre, perhaps, but that youth and vigour
(and that glamorous wife) had cast a glow. Now, in
hindsight, that glow grew rosy as, with the eager
encouragement of his widow Jackie – still young
and beautiful – America mourned the passing of
'Camelot' – the name of the court of the mythical
King Arthur, of course, and of a Broadway musical
that had recently celebrated it. There was elegiac
regret for a Kennedy White House that came to
be seen as a place of chivalric courtesy, idealism
and decency.

PICTURED HERE:
TONKIN TRICKERY
A US Navy photo shows a North Vietnamese motor torpedo boat allegedly attacking the USS *Maddox*, 2 August 1964. All may be fair in love and Cold War, but the Gulf of Tonkin incident was something special in cynicism. It gained President Lyndon B. Johnson the free hand he had been seeking, though.

LEFT:
MAO'S MUSHROOM CLOUD
Time waits for no superpower. On 16 October 1964, China tested its first atom bomb in the remotest reaches of Xinjiang's Taklamakan Desert. Life had just become that bit more complicated for the United States – and the Soviet Union.

OPPOSITE:
SAVING LIVES
US Marines engage the enemy in Santo Domingo, Dominican Republic, 1965. One has pushed a child under his jeep for safety. Given the dangerous anarchy prevailing, the Marine's humanitarian role was not entirely bogus. Nevertheless, the Johnson administration was eager to ensure that stability was restored in a way that suited them.

COLEGIO MARIA AUXILIADORA
2C2126

THE FALSE FLAG OF FREEDOM

To Kennedy's successor, Lyndon B. Johnson, fell the responsibility of managing America's involvement in the ongoing Vietnam conflict. Until now, that involvement had been heavy but indirect (materiel, supplies, intelligence and training). Even so, it seemed, the South was losing. The president's hands were tied, though. He knew he couldn't get congressional support for an extension of his commitment – certainly if it might mean American lives being lost. He saw his chance the following year, though. On 1 August, supporting South Vietnamese speedboat attacks on mainland coastal installations, an American destroyer, the USS *Maddox*, lay off the North Vietnamese island of Hon Me. As a trio of smaller North Vietnamese vessels approached to investigate, the crew of the *Maddox* felt spooked. Calling up air support, they opened fire themselves, badly damaging the Vietnamese boats. A single machine-gun round was subsequently dug out of the destroyer's superstructure.

A further 'attack' two days later in the same area seems to have been entirely imaginary. By now, a second destroyer had arrived by way of reinforcement. Both crews appear to have mistaken the sonar-sound of their own turbines for those of approaching torpedoes. Within an hour, however, the captain of the *Maddox*, John J. Herrick, had calmed down sufficiently to send home the message: 'ENTIRE ACTION LEAVES MANY DOUBTS'.

Not, however, in the minds of the president and his advisers. As repackaged for the Western media, this became a story of 'unprovoked' attacks on US vessels quietly minding their own business in international waters. In the ensuing outrage, Johnson was able to unilaterally push through Congress a special resolution allowing him to take military action without reference to elected representatives.

Massive 'retaliatory' airstrikes were launched: America was now officially a combatant in Vietnam. Four years later, 'LBJ' himself would acknowledge that the 'Gulf of Tonkin incident' had never taken place: 'Those damn stupid sailors were just shooting at flying fish.'

CONFUSION IN THE CARIBBEAN

Even before the Cold War had started, US support for unsavoury strongmen in the Caribbean had been an established tradition. Rafael Trujillo had been among the worst. It had been with America's tacit backing that, in 1931, he'd seized power and set up a one-party state in the Dominican Republic.

The usual defence of dictators is that they get things done. In 1937, Trujillo had dealt with the problem of illegal immigration by Haitians across his western border (among other things, a threat to his policy of 'whitening' the Dominican Republic) by massacring up to 15,000. In the years that followed, many hundreds of Dominicans had been killed by the executioners and torturers of 'the Goat'.

The dictator himself was dogged by personal accusations of rape and murder. Trujillo's bloody waywardness had come to embarrass even the United States. Some had traced the hand of the CIA in his 1961 assassination.

ON PARADE
President Johnson hangs on to a hand rail at the back of a jeep as he reviews American troops at Cam Ranh Bay, 1966. During his brief stay at the base in South Vietnam, the chief executive decorated several soldiers for their courage in battle.

CRBD
HQ-2

Even so, they missed him when he'd gone, as his country spiralled into anarchy and faction-fighting. The Cuban example obviously loomed large. What if a leftist faction should prevail and the Dominican domino fall? In 1963, some semblance of order had been restored with the inauguration of the country's first democratically elected president, Juan Bosch – but two years later he'd been ousted in a military coup. In 1965, when the new president, Donald Reid Cabral, was overthrown by Bosch supporters, civil war broke out. America sent in the Marines, restoring calm and organizing fresh elections at which a man more to their liking – Joaquín Balaguer – was brought to power.

Elsewhere in the Caribbean, the outlook was more reassuring for the United States. The Somoza dynasty had Nicaragua under control. It had been of founder Anastasio Somoza García, dictator since 1937, that Franklin D. Roosevelt had reputedly observed: 'He may be a sonofabitch, but he's our sonofabitch'. After his assassination in 1956, the sonofabitch's son Luis Somoza Debayle had carried on his work. He'd died of a heart attack in 1963 but a couple of client politicians had kept the presidential seat warm. In 1967, Anastasio Somoza's youngest son, Anastasio Somoza Debayle would take charge.

In Guatemala, Carlos Castillo Armas had been assassinated in 1957 but the country was in safe anti-communist hands under Óscar Mendoza Azurdia. In Honduras, the democratically elected President Ramón Villeda Morales had been toppled in a 1963 coup, making way for a military junta that caused Washington no concerns. Haiti might be a bloodbath under François Duvalier or 'Papa Doc' but at least there was no likelihood of any leftist subversion there.

THUNDERSTORM

The executive powers President Johnson had secured after the Gulf of Tonkin incident hadn't freed him from political constraints. While he had now been able to commit some 60,000 troops to help shore up a faltering South Vietnamese regime, he knew American casualties had to be kept to a minimum. Hence the appeal of Operation *Rolling Thunder*, an intense and protracted aerial bombardment of North Vietnam, its industries and infrastructure, and its communications links, both with the guerrillas in the South and the outside world.

The raids began in March 1965, and by the end of the year over 40,000 tons of high explosive had been dropped. The operation's effectiveness was already being questioned, though. Not only were the Vietnamese putting up a more effective than expected defence, with their Soviet-supplied MiG fighters, surface-to-air missiles and early-warning radar systems, but they were more resilient than anticipated under the attack. Still concerned to contain the conflict, moreover, commanders ordered that the main urban centres should be avoided.

While this made sense in both humanitarian and political terms, it limited the impact of the bombing – and forced aircrews to take greater risks seeking out more specific sensitive targets.

RED RUBBERNECKERS
On 29 May 1965, the UK's Queen Elizabeth II paid an official visit to West Berlin with her husband Prince Philip. East German border guards look on from a distance here from atop the Berlin Wall.

ROLLING THUNDER
Pounding North Vietnam and the Ho Chi Minh Trail from the air allowed the United States to maximize destruction to transport infrastructure without committing forces on the ground. But with Soviet materiel and technical support, the North Vietnamese were able to mount impressively effective resistance and the operation had to be abandoned after three years.

USAF
USAF

UOZ FBDXN
9

INTO ACTION
US troops arrive at Cam Ranh Base, on Vietnam's southern coast, prior to deployment in-country, July 1965. Johnson had concluded their presence was necessary, the arm's-length support his predecessors had confined themselves to having proven insufficient. Under twofold pressure from its own Viet Cong guerrillas and their North Vietnamese supporters, the resistance of the Republic of Vietnam was fading fast.

ABOVE TOP:
WAR WEARY
An exhausted US soldier of the 173rd Airborne Division is helped across a wasteland in War Zone D after the Battle for Zulu Zulu, 1966. The commitment of troops to Vietnam was already taking its toll on young American men – soon it would exact one from the politicians who had sent them there.

ABOVE LOWER:
CRUISING CALM
Guerrillas slip through reedbeds on their way to mount a surprise attack on US positions in Dong Thap Muoi, South Vietnam. Even with Soviet support, the Viet Cong were massively outgunned by their American opponents, but they had the advantage that they knew every inch, every contour of their home countryside.

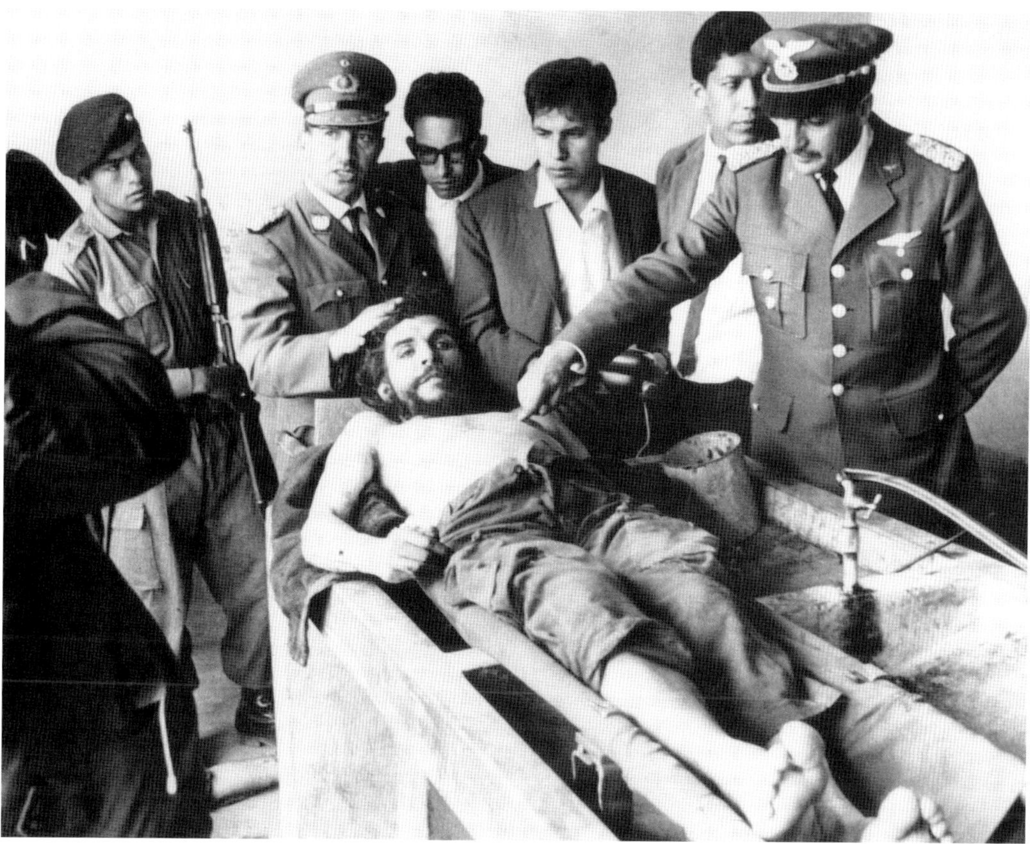

If aircrews felt frustrated, soldiers on the
ground felt even worse. Their fight against
the Viet Cong was greatly hindered by the
guerrillas' ability to blend in with the local
population (to which they of course belonged).
It made a nonsense of the nominal effort
to 'win hearts and minds'. Clearing areas of
countryside to create 'free-fire zones' saved lives
but uprooted communities and created deep
resentment. Furthermore, as discipline broke
down, atrocities were committed

Hearts and minds were being lost at home as
well. Reared in relative affluence and brought
up to believe that their country was a beacon

MARTYR AND MYTH
'Shoot, coward!' Ernesto 'Che' Guevara had told the
soldier who had come to execute him after his capture
in Bolivia. 'You are only going to kill a man.' He was
of course actually going to bring an icon into being.
Hundreds of villagers came to see the revolutionary's
body, displayed here at a nearby hospital.

of democracy, idealistic students were growing disenchanted. They saw the oppressive actions being carried out in freedom's name in Vietnam; the more enterprising among them read up on recent and historic foreign policy.

Thousands marched against the war – and for a wide array of other causes. Dismay at America's role in Vietnam seemed to be bringing other wrongs into sharper focus, in everything from sexuality to race. Building through the 1960s, the civil rights movement had suffered a grievous blow – and gained enormous new momentum – with the assassination of Martin Luther King Jr. in Memphis, in April 1968. That year's Democratic National Convention, held in Chicago, was besieged by protesters – who were then put down in what was described as a 'police riot'.

BELOW:
REJOICING AND RELIEF
Troops bar flag-waving students from approaching President Sukarno's summer palace in Bogor, after news of an abortive communist coup, 1965. Having led his country's freedom struggle since the days of Dutch colonial occupation, Sukarno enjoyed immense popularity in Indonesia.

LEFT:
A DICTATOR IN WAITING
Sukarno's Defence Minister Suharto does his official duty by attending the funeral of former Prime Minister Sutan Sjahrir, in April 1966. Within a year he would have toppled his boss and seized power himself. His cruel, kleptomaniac reign was to be a disaster for Indonesia but a boon to his US backers in the Cold War.

SIX-DAY WAR
Israeli soldiers storm an
Arab position in the course
of 1967's Six-Day War. The
ease with which they rolled over
their enemy would astound
the world and leave the Soviet
Union, whose loyal clients the
Arab combatants had been,
looking badly diminished on
the global stage.

ВПЕРЕД, К ПОБЕДЕ КОММУНИЗМА!

SHOW OF STRENGTH
Moscow, 7 November 1967. The frowning face of Lenin looks down from the banner-draped façade of the GUM department store as ballistic missiles are paraded through Red Square. Displays of military might were part of the pageantry of the Soviet Union. Here, however, a special effort is being made to mark the 50th anniversary of the Revolution of 1917.

RADICAL CHEEK

Peace protesters taunt a line of military police outside the Pentagon, Washington D.C. By 1968, 'student radicalism' was a thing. While only the tiniest minority ever conspired against the state, many more campaigned, for everything from banning the bomb to Black civil rights; from withdrawal from Vietnam to women's liberation.

LEFT:

TET OFFENSIVE

A wounded US Marine receives treatment during the Tet Offensive at Hue, February 1968. The war was starting to seem unwinnable for the United States. Not so much here, where the NVA and Viet Cong were being beaten back, but on a home front that felt bombarded with bad news. If it wasn't the endless stream of husbands, sons, brothers and boyfriends coming back in body bags, it was the stories of atrocities committed by US troops.

CRISIS IN CAPITALISM

Soviet commentators were understandably eager to represent America's troubles as a 'crisis in capitalism'. Perhaps it was. But they were in no position to judge, given the way their rule had been unravelling in Czechoslovakia. Again, young idealists had been to blame. Well, reasonably young idealists: though 48 when elected to the Communist Party leadership, Alexander Dubček was the merest stripling by the gerontocratic standards of the Eastern Bloc.

And he certainly mobilized the young. Calling for significant democratization and decentralization of the state, Dubček offered Czechoslovakia 'socialism with a human face'. They would remain loyal members of the Warsaw Pact, but go their own way within that. Censorship would be eased and the arts encouraged. It was all undoubtedly calculated to appeal to the young and optimistic – those who didn't remember East Berlin 1953 or Budapest 1956. Students turned out in their thousands to march in its support. (To this extent, you could see parallels with the US 'counterculture'.) But many older Czechs and Slovaks seem to have sympathized with the reformist cause – even if they wondered a little fearfully where it was all going to end.

RED ARMY OCCUPATION

The Soviet leadership certainly seem to have remembered Berlin and Budapest and the opprobrium that their interventions there had brought. They tried hard to talk Dubček out of his plans. When he wouldn't back down, though, they didn't flinch but once more (on 20–1 August 1968) mounted an invasion. Czechoslovakia wasn't going to be allowed its freedom.

PREVIOUS PAGES & RIGHT:
PRAGUE SPRING
The 'Prague Spring' gives way
to a dismal autumn, the centre
of the city become a battlefield.
But the status of the Soviets
as occupiers is at least now
clear. Czechoslovakia's great
experiment had begun on
5 January with the election
of the reformist Alexander
Dubček as first secretary of
the Communist Party. His bid
to democratize the country
had gone down so badly in
Moscow that the Soviet leader
Leonid Brezhnev had sent in a
600,000-strong invasion force.

'HEAP CHAOS UPON CHAOS!'
'It is right to rebel,' said
Mao, who shored up his own
position by mobilizing Chinese
youth against an imaginary
establishment of 'bourgeois
reactionaries' in the Cultural
Revolution. 'I was Chairman
Mao's Dog,' said his wife
Jiang Qing (left here with her
husband's deputy Zhou Enlai).
'What he said "bite" I bit.'
Millions died in a spree
of violence and destruction.

FLIGHT
DECK
OFFICER

1970s

On 3 January 1970, a curtain came down on the ebullient show the 'Swinging Sixties' had been as the Beatles recorded their last song. At least, most of the Beatles did: John Lennon was too occupied with his artistic differences with Paul McCartney and his new relationship (and artistic collaboration) with Yoko Ono. George Harrison's song, entitled 'I Me Mine', was a musing on the Indian mystic philosophy that had so enthralled him. But, listening later, fans couldn't help hearing a swipe at the egotistic individualism that had pulled the group apart. A few years later, the American journalist Tom Wolfe was to speak of the 1970s as the 'Me Decade'.

A popular consensus had been forming for some time that those born in the 'Baby Boom' that had followed World War II were marked out from previous generations by their self-absorption. They had indeed in a great many cases grown up in relative affluence and with unprecedented opportunities for leisure.

OPPOSITE:
BIRD OVERBOARD
Operation *Frequent Wind* marked America's final, frantic withdrawal from Vietnam. Thousands of US personnel and local civilian staff were evacuated from Saigon during 29–30 April 1975. Here, a helicopter is tipped over the side of the USS *Okinawa* to free up deck-space so further flights can land.

BORDER FIGHT
Private First Class Steve Morrison, of Louisville, Kentucky, fires a grenade towards a suspected enemy position in the A Shau Valley, west of Hue. The Ho Chi Minh Trail crossed the border a little way north of here, so it was frequently the scene of heavy fighting.

SEEK-AND-DESTROY MISSION
US soldiers tumble from a helicopter near My Tho in South Vietnam's Mekong Delta, 1971. Having had intelligence of Viet Cong activity, they will try to find the guerrillas, eliminate them and then immediately withdraw. These were the basic, everyday tactics of the United States in Vietnam.

As the 1960s gave way to the 1970s, though, it seemed the silent majority were quietly wearying of the war. The My Lai massacre of March 1968 had shown them a side of US military action they had not been comfortable with. The fight to uphold democracy wasn't supposed to involve the gang-rape of civilian women or the killing and mutilation of young children. Nor the death and incapacitation of so many of their own sons.

Nor, for that matter, was it supposed to end in anything other than a speedy US victory. This, successive administrations had signally failed to produce. In part, the problem had been the way that news was managed in a democracy. The Tet Offensive mounted by the NVA and VC in January 1968 had been emphatically repulsed. It had felt like a defeat for Americans, though. So assiduously had government spokesmen striven to foster the impression that the war was all but won that the fact that the communists had been able to orchestrate an attack on this sort of scale had created consternation.

ARAB ALTERNATIVES?

How different from the way in which America's Middle Eastern ally Israel had seen off its Arab enemies just a few years before! In 1967's so-called Six-Day War, Israel had sent the combined forces of Jordan, Syria and Egypt packing and secured the territory of Sinai, along with the West Bank of the Jordan River, the Gaza Strip and (up on the border with Syria) the Golan Heights. Americans had looked on in admiration – and increasing envy.

Yet if these gains enhanced Israeli security in the short term they also guaranteed the continuation of the Middle Eastern conflict, since their losses naturally rankled with the Arab states. Furthermore, any attempts at finding a negotiated settlement were going to be complicated by the presence in these border zones of a Palestinian population forced out of Israel in the

fighting (the First Arab–Israeli War) that had followed that nation's foundation in 1947.

For the moment, though, the mood in Israel was upbeat. The Arab world was left to lick its wounds and look for a realistic way of moving forward which, at least for an Egypt under the leadership of Nasser's sometime lieutenant and now successor Anwar Sadat, meant a break with the Soviet Union.

Though taken up now through much of the Middle East, the 'Arab Nationalism' Nasser had espoused was confusingly named. It made sense only if you appreciated that the 'nation' concerned was that of the Arab (not, say, of the Syrian, Egyptian, Libyan or Jordanian). By most normal standards, then, it was transnational and had much less in common with the stereotypical nationalist movements of the right than with the internationalist ideologies of the left. This (along with the political practicalities – the United States had sponsored Israel since its foundation) had determined the Arab Nationalists' alignment with the Soviet Bloc.

Sadat's 'Corrective Revolution' represented a break with the Soviet Union, both in diplomacy and domestic politics. Having purged the most loyally Nasserist officials and expelled the Soviet advisers his predecessor had invited in, he set about democratizing Egypt. Disbanding the country's secret police, he allowed other ideological voices to be raised – and most notably, those calling for a religious dimension to the country's government.

AGAINST THE ODDS
Bangladeshi militiamen stand defiant, 1971. Cold War considerations led the United States to turn a blind eye to the brutality of West Pakistan's efforts to suppress the Bengali separatist movement in East Pakistan (now Bangladesh). Anything up to 3 million were killed and up to 400,000 girls and women raped in a systematic programme of oppression. But Bangladesh was finally to win its freedom.

NGLADESH
ATION FORCES
POST OFFICE No 14
বাংলাদেশ পোষ্ট অফিস ১৪

SAFETY IN NUMBERS
Muammar Gadaffi of Libya
(seated centre) signs the
short-lived 'Federation of
Arab Republics' into being
with Egypt's Anwar Sadat
(left) and Syria's Hafez
al-Assad (right), in 1971. A
succession of attempts were
made to shuffle the pack of
Arab countries and come up
with wider unions. Egypt and
Syria had joined briefly before
as the United Arab Republic
(1958–71); Libya and Tunisia
would consider merging with
Morocco and Algeria in 1974.

THE MATCH OF THE CENTURY

Communist orthodoxy was firm in the belief that their system didn't just offer a better life but could scientifically engineer human improvement. Physically, in the sporting field; mentally in the academy. Or in chess, which contained elements of both. Since the 1920s, a string of Soviet grandmasters had amazed the world, combining individual brilliance with team spirit and discipline. The 1972 World Chess Championship pitched the latest of these, Boris Spassky (left), against a flamboyant challenger, the Brooklyn-born Bobby Fischer. A maverick – not to say a prima donna – Fischer presented as a parody of American individualism. But he had what it took to win the title for the West.

GRINDING OUT VICTORY
An Israeli tank traverses an empty wasteland somewhere in the Golan Heights: a visual metaphor for the country's achievements in 1973. Israel ground out its victory, but it took so long and exacted such a price that it took much of the lustre off its earlier triumph in the Six-Day War.

A Marxist-inflected Arab Nationalism had seen no place in the political process for those pushing the 'opium of the people'. Sadat's benevolence towards the Muslim Brotherhood was not entirely motivated by tolerance and generosity. He saw their conservatism as a brake against any socialist backsliding.

YOM KIPPUR WAR

Indirectly, his reforms – along with the authority he was beginning to assert in the Arab world – could be seen as advancing the interests of the West in the Cold War. That he led the Arabs into another war with Israel, attacking on the Jewish holy day of penitence, Yom Kippur (6 October 1973), was less welcome to the West. But the inconclusive outcome suited them. After impressive initial gains, which helped banish the humiliation of 1967, the Arabs were contained. However, the Israelis didn't win convincingly enough to feel triumphant.

THE STORM SPREADS

In Vietnam, meanwhile, the Americans were still having a torrid time. Try as they might, they could not suppress the NVA or VC. What should have been a profitable point of application – the communists' supply lines and main depots and bases – seemed invulnerable because for the most part they weren't in Vietnam at all. Further north, the Ho Chi Minh Trail ran largely through the forests of Laos, just across the border from Vietnam. Further south, its route lay through Cambodia, with whose King Sihanouk the communists now had an improbable friendship. Having expressed increasing doubts about America's handling of the conflict in his next-door country, he had been ousted in 1970 by his prime minister, Lon

Nol, whom the State Department felt would be more biddable. From that time on, from a home in exile, he would wage a bitter civil war against Lon Nol's dictatorship, in alliance with the Khmer Rouge.

America's big B-52 bombers had been left idle by the abandonment of Operation *Rolling Thunder* in 1968. Since 1969, though, they had been used to bomb targets along the Ho Chi Minh Trail in Cambodia. Operation *Menu* had been undeclared. Now, however, Washington broke cover with its aerial bombardment under Operation *Freedom Deal*.

In the three years from 1970, US planes dropped a quarter of a million tons of bombs on the country (far more, notoriously, than they'd dropped on Japan during World War II). Add in the ordnance dropped during *Menu* and the total comes to something approaching half a million tons. Despite assurances to the king, the raids killed tens of thousands of Cambodian civilians. Similar raids were launched in Laos. As in Vietnam itself, the pilots' sightlines were cleared by the dropping of defoliants like Agent Orange, which laid waste the land – and left a legacy of sickness. The health problems the populations of all these countries suffered have continued to this day. Fortunately for the Nixon administration, the press took little interest.

But it didn't seem to matter how apocalyptic the American attack was: they couldn't make serious headway against the communists.

MENDING FENCES
Richard Nixon takes time out for sightseeing on the Great Wall of China in the course of his official visit, February 1972. A surprise to the whole world, the trip wrong-footed Moscow at a time when it was at odds with Beijing in the aftermath of the Sino–Soviet split.

THE 'SPARROW FROM MINSK'
Slight and pretty, and just
17 at the time of the 1972
Summer Olympics in Munich,
the Belarusian gymnast Olga
Korbut thrilled the world.
Each of her three gold medals
was a triumph for Soviet
'soft power' – especially
her performance on the
uneven bars: her trademark
'Korbut Flip' (a back-flip
made from a standing
position on the higher bar)
is highly dangerous and was
subsequently banned.

The NVA had the advantage (however dubious) of representing a totalitarian state that didn't have to account to its citizens for any reverses or for casualties. The Viet Cong had the flexibility guerrillas have that regular forces don't (and, it seemed, the sympathy and support of the rural population).

The hyperactivity of America's bombers helped mask the slow but steady scaling-down of the US commitment on the ground, under a policy of 'Vietnamization' that started in earnest in 1970.

Increasingly, the task of fighting the communists was to be handed over to the South Vietnamese themselves, with ample amounts of US assistance in theory – and up to a point in practice, too. However, by 1973, the Republic of Vietnam, impossibly beleaguered, was forced to reach an accommodation with its enemies at the Paris Peace Talks. A general ceasefire was signed between South Vietnam, the United States, the North Vietnamese and the Viet Cong. This would have been a favourable outcome if the United States hadn't been the only party to 'honour' the agreement. It promptly removed what remained of its fighting forces in the country – even as the NVA and VC resumed their operations, with barely a pause; while South Vietnamese government forces were left to struggle on unaided.

REALITY CHECK

Great powers have always been perfidious. The United States could hardly be said to have committed any special historic iniquity in abandoning a loyal ally in its hour of desperate need. Even so, its decision to up and leave and let the dominoes fall where they might did nevertheless represent a significant departure from Cold War precedent.

It was of a piece with the new administration's thinking, though. Since the start of his term in 1969, Richard Nixon had tried to take a little of the chill out of the Cold War. This action was not derived from idealistic motives but from what he saw as a realistic recognition that somehow the rival camps were going to have to find a way to get along. Schooled by his security adviser (and, from 1973, his secretary of state), Henry Kissinger, he pursued a policy of detente (literally 'relaxation') towards the Soviet Union. Kissinger made a point of his realism (some said his amorality) in diplomatic relations. The United States should be guided by its own self-interest, not by philanthropic concern for the world at large.

SABOTAGING SALVADOR

There was certainly no sign of philanthropic concern for the people of Chile under Salvador Allende's government at this time. True, Allende was a Marxist by his own avowal; but it was true too that he'd been democratically elected, according to the constitution of his country, having won a congressional run-off between tied candidates in 1970. Once in power, he had set about leading his countrymen and -women down what he called 'the Chilean path to socialism', raising minimum wages, improving healthcare and nationalizing banks and mining companies.

MARXIST MARTYRDOM

Santiago's La Moneda Palace burns on 11 September 1973, and with it, Chilean democracy goes up in smoke. Rebel air force pilots had hit the president's residence with some 19 rockets. Allende himself stayed doggedly, if ultimately pointlessly, at his post.

Allende also inaugurated a programme of land reform, taking unworked tracts from big landowners to be worked by smaller farmers. As popular as these policies appeared to be with the mass of Chile's poor, they went down very badly with the old elite.

And, of course, with Washington. The CIA had tried hard to prevent Allende being elected in the first place. Now it worked tirelessly to destabilize his country. Following a familiar pattern, he may well have felt more or less compelled by US hostility to enter into a closer relationship with the USSR than he would have liked. Acting on Nixon's order that they 'make the economy scream' in Chile, US officials worked with right-wing groups to create disruption. Especially effective was the 'strike' by 'truck drivers' (really small- and mid-sized haulage contractors rather than 'workers'), which ultimately brought the country to a halt.

AUGUSTO'S OUTRAGE

On 11 September 1973, the Chilean Army's commander-in-chief, Augusto Pinochet, led the armed forces in a coup. In surreal scenes, tanks took to the streets of Santiago. Planes attacked the presidential palace from the air while soldiers stormed it. Allende remained in his office, defiant to the last. He died at his desk. He is believed to have shot himself rather than be captured alive, though doubts have lingered over whether he was really murdered.

A SUITABLE SEND-OFF

Not until 1990 was Salvador Allende to receive a fitting funeral. His body was disinterred from its unmarked grave, then carried in state through the streets to Santiago's national cathedral. After a commemorative mass, he was laid to rest with the other presidents of Chile.

INTEGRITY IN EXILE
The German writer Heinrich Böll welcomes Aleksandr Solzhenitsyn to his home in Langenbroich, West Germany, 1974. The Nobel Prize winner had, in novels like *One Day in the Life of Ivan Denisovich* (1962) and *The First Circle* (1968) catalogued the human rights abuses of the Soviet system. He had now been stripped of his citizenship and expelled.

A DIRTY DEAL?

The two sides thrash out the detail on the Paris Peace Accords (or, to give them their full title, the 'Agreement on Ending the War and Restoring Peace in Viet Nam') in January 1973. Despite the sober atmosphere and the portentous statements traded by the two sides, South Vietnam would come to feel that the conference had merely given cover for the United States to cut and run from its commitments. The mastermind of US foreign policy in the early 1970s, Kissinger had become a hate-figure for the American left. If his conduct of the Vietnam peace talks belied the assumption that he was an out-and-out 'warmonger', it did show just how ruthless his 'realism' could be.

VICTORS
Jubilant Khmer Rouge fighters enter the Cambodian capital, Phnom Penh, 17 April 1975. But the mood in the country was very quickly to turn sour. Pol Pot's 'peace' would be far worse than any war.

OPPOSITE:
DUSK OR DAWN?
Freedom at last for the people of Saigon or the start of a repressive nightmare? Troops of the North Vietnamese Army arrive in Saigon, 30 April 1975. Inevitably, many here had worked with the Americans through the decades of their presence. They naturally feared being branded as collaborators.

Pinochet took charge in Chile, beginning his reign with mass executions. Thousands of 'subversives' were rounded up and herded into the National Stadium. Up to 4,000 people were summarily executed there. More than 130,000 more would be snatched over the next three years. Killings, 'disappearances', torture and other human rights abuses would continue through Pinochet's 17 years in power.

IMPLOSIONS

But Chile's tragedy and the bloody farce Vietnam had been slowly sinking into seemed like so many 'noises off' to Americans just now. It was shocking to find that the Nixon presidential campaign had (in 1972) organized a break-in at its Democratic rivals' office in Washington's Watergate Building to steal documents and wiretap phones. But, as the cliché had it, if the crime was bad, the cover-up was worse. The list of luminaries implicated only seemed to grow and grow until, in August 1974, President Nixon himself was forced to resign.

American influence in Southeast Asia was also crumbling, the Cold War balance swinging communism's way. Effectively abandoned after the Paris Accords (which North Vietnam and the Viet Cong pretty much ignored), South Vietnam kept up an increasingly futile rearguard action. More and more of its territory was occupied until April 1975 brought the enemy to the threshold of its capital, Saigon. Belatedly, in the final 24 hours, the Americans whisked 9,000 civilian staff and helpers away to safety, but many thousands more were left behind to face communist 're-education' or worse. The South Vietnamese countryside had been left devastated, over two thirds of its villages razed; 5 million hectares (12 million acres) of forest destroyed by defoliants.

KILLING FIELDS

By this time, Cambodia's Khmer Rouge had moved in to occupy Phnom Penh. Sihanouk and his supporters having outlived their usefulness, they were duly purged. But Pol Pot was only getting started. The leader of what was now 'Democratic Kampuchea' was a man in whom an obsession with ideological purity had become a murderous pathology. He viewed anyone with any sort of education as a threat and sent students and urban professionals to carry out forced labour in the countryside. Many tens of thousands were to be summarily executed out here in the 'Killing Fields'.

THE BITTER END
Civilian evacuees are helped on to a helicopter on the roof near the US Embassy, Saigon in the hours before the communist takeover of the city. Many thousands of local staff and helpers ended up being left behind to face their fates. America's exit was not just undignified, but bordered on the ethically unseemly.

'BATTLE OF RICE'
Many Vietnamese villagers were to squat like this amongst the smouldering ruins of their villages, destroyed by the Americans. This Cambodian woman owes her homelessness to the Viet Cong. The siting of the Ho Chi Minh Trail had made such peripheral actions inevitable. The conflict here boiled over in early 1974.

VILLAGE FIGHT
Cambodian troops defend the town of Kampong Cham from attempted encirclement by North Vietnamese and Viet Cong forces determined to keep open their supply lines to South Vietnam, at any cost.

HASTY EXIT
Cambodians look on from behind a perimeter fence as US officials and foreign nationals are scooped up unceremoniously from a school playing field after the fall of Phnom Penh in April 1975.

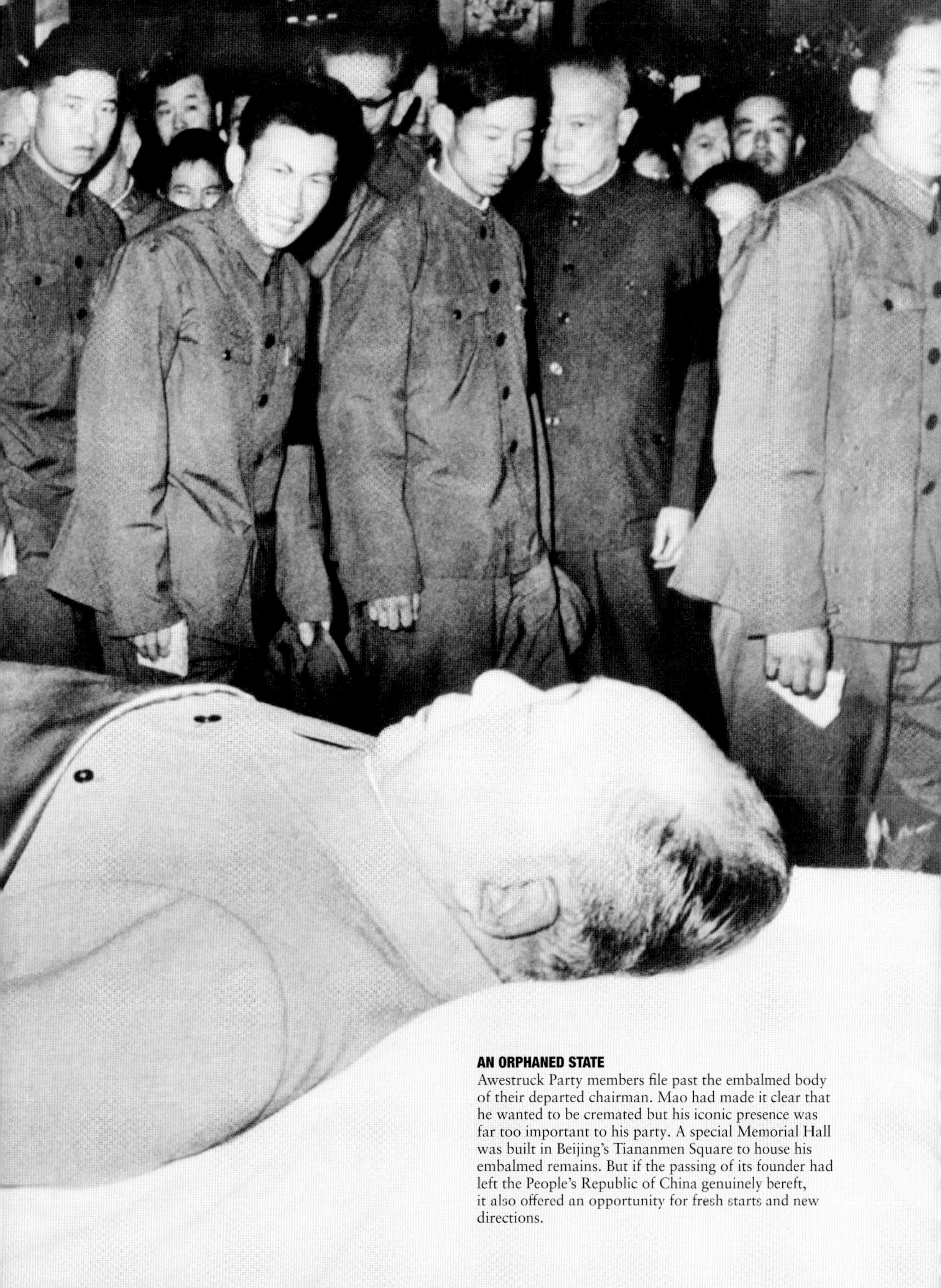

AN ORPHANED STATE
Awestruck Party members file past the embalmed body of their departed chairman. Mao had made it clear that he wanted to be cremated but his iconic presence was far too important to his party. A special Memorial Hall was built in Beijing's Tiananmen Square to house his embalmed remains. But if the passing of its founder had left the People's Republic of China genuinely bereft, it also offered an opportunity for fresh starts and new directions.

鄧小平副総理
黄華外交部長

園田外務大臣
福田総理大臣

Pol Pot's purist attitudes arguably reflected the influence of Mao, whose China was by now replacing the Soviet Union as key sponsor of the Khmer Rouge. Increasingly, indeed, the Cold War opposition in this part of Southeast Asia was taking second place as a driver of political events to the longer-term consequences of the Sino–Soviet split (p. 85). Kampuchea's nightmare was only to come to an end in 1977, when Soviet-backed Vietnam invaded and defeated the Khmer Rouge.

Cambodia's weren't the only killing fields. Indonesia's invasion of East Timor in 1975 sparked a long and bloody period of repression by Suharto's state. A Portuguese colony until just the year before, close as it was to Java, East Timor had its own distinct culture.

Indonesia's territorial ambitions meshed with US fears of a communist statelet springing up in a postcolonial power vacuum. Seen in those terms, Suharto's invasion had made sense. It didn't make any to the Timorese, though. Over a hundred thousand were killed in the fighting, the famine it brought with it, and the atrocities Indonesian forces inflicted.

AFRICAN CIVIL WARS

The savannahs of southern Africa saw their share of bloodshed, too. There were ghastly civil wars in Angola and Mozambique. These had started out as independence struggles but, the death of Portugal's elderly dictator António Salazar (1970) having led within a few years to his country's 'Carnation

FIGHTING TALK
Freedom fighters of Fretilin (the Revolutionary Front for an
Independent East Timor) are rallied by their founder – and
future president – José Ramos-Horta, October 1975.

FORGOTTEN COLONY
José Ramos-Horta (right) walks through the forest with a
Fretilin patrol, October 1975. A Portuguese possession until
just the year before, East Timor, a tiny nation, now faced what
amounted to recolonization by Suharto's Indonesia.

Revolution' and transition to democracy (1974), the rebels had found themselves pushing at an open door.

Independence came in 1975. In both countries, Marxist governments set up one-party states to which resistance was organized by right-wing militias. Inevitably, these conflicts were co-opted by the Cold War rivals. In Mozambique, the Soviets backed the government of the National Front for the Liberation of Mozambique (FRELIMO); the Americans the guerrillas of the Mozambican National Resistance (RENAMO).

In Angola, the Popular Movement for the Liberation of Angola (MPLA) had Soviet support; the rebel National Union for the Total Independence of Angola (UNITA) that of the United States.

NOT A TOY
The gun was a grim leveller, equipping a boy to do a man's job – physically, if not emotionally. This child soldier is serving with the leftist Angolan MPLA.

¡QUE VIVA LA REVOLUCIÓN!
Sandinista rebels ride in triumph through Managua ready to take power in 1979, the culmination of a 40-year campaign against successive Somoza presidents. Like Fidel Castro and his *compañeros* 40 years before, the Sandinistas brought an element of romance and colour to what could seem a drab and earnest left-wing cause.

STRIDING FORWARD
Flanked by fellow revolutionaries, Daniel Ortega walks through Managua in Nicaragua at the head of a triumphant people's march in 1979. The leader of the 'Junta of National Reconstruction', set up on the overthrow of Anastasio Somoza Debayle, Ortega was the most charismatic leader to have emerged on the international left since Fidel Castro. His programme of nationalization, land reform and redistribution of wealth would secure him the presidency, and the Sandinistas the government, in the 1985 elections.

CIA PLOTS

A much-needed moment of light relief came with the revelation (before the US Senate's Church Committee, 1975) of some of the CIA's more wayward plots against Fidel Castro. Ideas included sprinkling a depilatory on his microphone to make his trademark beard fall out, and an exploding cigar.

There had been less to laugh at in China. In his last decade, Mao had decided to jolt his people out of what he saw as their comfortable complacency with a 'Cultural Revolution'. Carried out by young, fanatical 'Red Guards', this spree of vandalism and mob violence had caused untold destruction and cost anything up to 10 million lives. Yet his personality cult had made Mao a literal legend in his own lifetime. So, his death in 1976 left the Chinese people lost. But some of their leaders saw the chance to take their country off on a different track. Economic reforms would be announced by Deng Xiaoping at the end of 1978.

The decade ended with Soviet troops being sent into Afghanistan where the USSR's client government was under threat from local guerrillas – mujahideen. If the situation showed the limits of Soviet authority, Moscow's prompt and forceful response underlined the power it was prepared to exercise in its 'backyard'.

A GLIMPSE OF THE FUTURE?
The Soviets' nemesis in Afghanistan, the mujahideen were also arguably an indication of the shape of strategic things to come. Not only would their victory confirm the 'small is beautiful' logic that had underlain the Viet Cong's, but they were driven by religious convictions the Cold War paradigm did not allow for.

AIMING HIGH
Government forces in Afghanistan had all the advantages of Soviet sponsorship – in training, equipment and supplies – but they struggled to match the commitment and resourcefulness of their foes. Here, mujahideen man a captured Soviet-made anti-aircraft machine gun.

AFGHAN ANXIETIES
Soviet soldiers, sent to support a Moscow-backed government that was coming under pressure in the country, make their wary way along a road in Afghanistan. Moscow feared that, at best, warring tribesmen would reduce the place to anarchy or, at worst, an unpredictable Islamic state would spring up on its southern border.

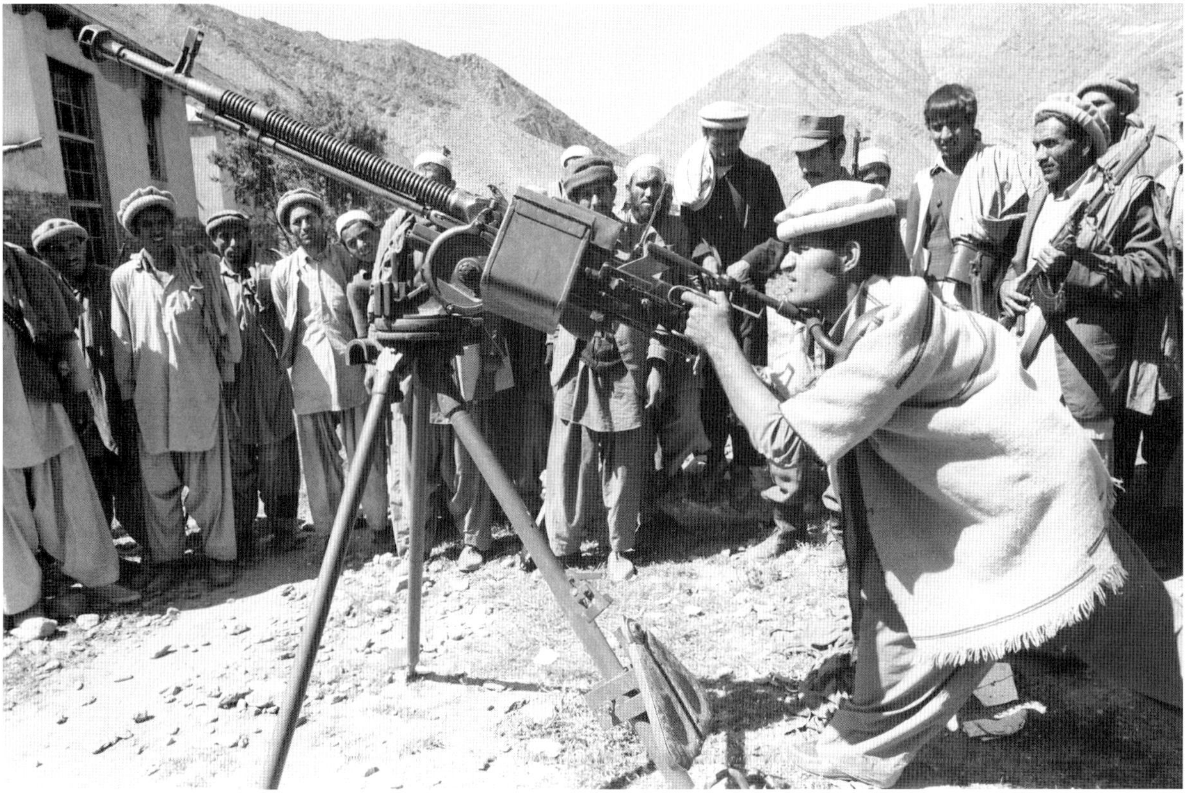

A POPE FOR POLAND
A year after his election,
Pope John Paul II made a
triumphant visit to his native
Poland. Born in Wadowice,
a clandestine seminarian in
Krakow during World War
II, Karol Wojtyla had been
ordained to the priesthood in
1946. He was described – by
both admirers and detractors
– as the 'Rock Star Pope'.
His trip to Poland wasn't just
about spiritual but also about
patriotic renewal, prompting
a powerful eruption of
national pride. Here, he
addresses a crowd from
the balcony of the Bishop's
residence in Gniezno.

U.S.S.R.
SUKS.

1980s

On 3 January 1980, back in the Oval Office after the New Year break, Jimmy Carter opened a new phase in the Cold War. His request to the US Senate that they hold fire (as it were) on approving the Strategic Arms Limitation Talks (SALT II) treaty was his administration's first real response to the Soviet invasion of Afghanistan. There would be plenty more. While much of it would be symbolic, it would still cut through.

The ill-feeling was to affect that February's Winter Olympics at Lake Placid, New York. The United States called for the cancellation of the Summer Olympic Games, to be held in Moscow later that year. Although the International Olympic Committee refused, the Americans' unilateral boycott overshadowed what the Soviets had hoped would be a triumphant showcasing of their collective talent and sporting prowess.

As disconcerting as the invasion of Afghanistan had been for the Americans, there was already a sense for the Soviets of maybe having overreached. Western commentators were already gloating that the war would be 'Russia's Vietnam'.

WINTER CHILL

American protesters at the Winter Olympics, Lake Placid, New York, register their anger over the Soviet invasion of Afghanistan and demand a boycott of the Moscow Games. Calls for this had already been building over the Soviet Union's record on human rights.

PARTY POOPED

The spectacular opening ceremony of the 1980 Summer Olympic Games in Moscow showed that the Soviet Union had lost none of its ability to put on a totalitarian party on the old scale. Thanks to the Western boycott, however, it all fell rather flat.

There was no doubt a good deal of wishful thinking in this claim. At the same time, it sounded just convincing enough to cause concern in Moscow.

FAITH, HOPE AND SOLIDARITY

In so far as it had concerned itself with politics at all, the Catholic Church had always taken the conservative side. It appreciated the protection of the powerful and the donations of the wealthy. It also feared the influence of a progressivism that it saw as encouraging irreverence at best and atheism at worst. So it had been in the Cold War. The capitalist countries might arguably have been materialistic in their consumer culture but communism was avowedly 'materialist' in its thinking.

At a popular level, Catholics had for some time been seeing the superpower-struggle in religious terms. They had found inspiration in the devotion (some would say the 'cult') of Our Lady of Fátima. Appearing to a group of children in the little Portuguese village in 1917, the Virgin Mary had apparently prophesied that a godless Russia would before long be 'consecrated' to her 'Immaculate Heart'. Inevitably, in the Cold War era, this prophesy had been interpreted as predicting the conquest and conversion of the godless USSR.

Not that other views of the world situation weren't available. The Church was vast and its scriptures rich and complex. Hence the hold exercised on idealistic priests and nuns in Latin America by what became known as 'Liberation Theology'. Taking a line through Christ's outspoken advocacy of the poor and uncompromising condemnation of the rich, they had reinvented him as a revolutionary. Movements like Sandinismo had been bolstered by their support.

In the context of a communist Poland, though, Catholicism's very conservatism made it revolutionary. And its cause had been lifted powerfully by Pope John Paul II's visit (pp. 170–1). Many in the country had clung to their Catholicism as an aspect of a national

identity they saw as having been suppressed under Soviet domination.

Among them were working-class men and women of just the kind for whom socialism nominally existed – and for whom religion (Marx had maintained) simply didn't care. Men like Lech Walesa, who in August 1980 led a walk-out at the Lenin Shipyard in Gdansk.

Sparked off by what the workers saw as the unjust dismissal of a female comrade, the strike at the Lenin Shipyard had prompted sympathy actions across Poland. Beyond their more specific demands was an important principle: the right of workers to organize at all. Strikes were illegal in the Iron Curtain countries. Since socialism supposedly represented government-by-the-workers anyway, the communist states didn't recognize their citizens' rights to unionize.

OPPOSITE:
AN END AND A BEGINNING
At a mass meeting of 31 August 1981, Lech Walesa tells a cheering crowd of workers that the strike is over: the government had signed the 'Gdansk Agreement', recognizing their right to unionize. But Solidarnosc as a wider movement was just beginning. It would have reverberations throughout the Iron Curtain countries.

OVERLEAF:
USING A SLEDGEHAMMER …?
Polish soldiers stop a man on the street to check his papers (left) while one of their comrades goes into a shop to see who's there. Martial law was effective up to a point. It put an end to open protest. But, in forcing the freedom movement underground, it arguably only stored up trouble for the future.

NICZY

TED STATES
MER

A SHIELD IN SPACE
President Reagan reports on progress in the United States' Strategic Defense Initiative (SDI), January 1987, since his initial announcement of the plan in 1984. By this time, he was bluffing. Government scientists seem to have been warning him that technological advances on which the programme would crucially depend in some cases still lay several years off. The evidence is that the Soviets suspected this. They certainly didn't curtail their intercontinental ballistic missile programme. Even so, the very idea of the 'Star Wars' system had upped the ante. How were the Soviets to deal with even a partially successful SDI?

Poland's Solidarnosc ('Solidarity') free trade union and the wider movement it sparked off was to be brutally put down, from 13 December 1981, when communist leader General Wojciech Jaruzelski declared martial law. But not before its message of courage and hope had inspired the world.

A SHIELD IN SPACE

Ronald Reagan became president of the United States in 1981. The former film actor was personally genial but politically right wing – aggressively so, in his attitude to the Soviet Union, it seemed: in a speech of March 1983 he branded it an 'evil empire'. Neither his own media nor the Soviet premier, Yuri Andropov, knew how seriously to take him when, in another speech only a few weeks later, he mused aloud about a weapons system he said was in development that would remove the risk of nuclear war.

An integrated system of satellites, lasers, missiles and other advanced weapons, it would allow ICBMs (intercontinental ballistic missiles) to be intercepted before they could threaten America. Unsurprisingly, the idea caught the imagination of the press. Inevitably, it became known as 'Star Wars', from the sci-fi movie franchise of the time.

TIT FOR TAT
The Los Angeles Olympics, 1984, were naturally boycotted by the Eastern Bloc. Here, American fans send facetious greetings. However, the sabotaging of successive Games had been a real tragedy for athletes and the integrity of the Olympics had been put at risk.

O RUSSIA WITH LOVE!
AVING A GREAT TIME,
ISH YOU WERE HERE!
FROM ALL OF US

КАСПАРОВ

BATTLE OF THE BOARD

In 1984, the Soviets got the chance of revenge for Fischer's defeat of Spassky when Anatoly Karpov faced off against fellow Russian Garry Kasparov in the World Chess Championship. Karpov had dominated world chess for a decade; at first, the challenger struggled to wear him down. He began to make headway, but only very slowly and finally, after five long months and 48 games, the match was cancelled. Given that Karpov had still been leading, the decision was controversial – the more so after Kasparov won the following year's rematch.

Even allowing for exaggeration in Reagan's claims, SDI was transformative in scope. It certainly caused consternation in the Soviet Bloc. Andropov didn't even go through the motions of pretending he wasn't spooked. The initiative would have a destabilizing impact, he warned; it was a menace to world peace. And, despite assurances that they were going to come under its protective umbrella, it caused a degree of nervousness in the United States' European allies, too.

Six months later, Soviet fighters shot down a Korean Airlines passenger jet flying from Anchorage, Alaska, to Seoul, which had strayed into their airspace in the Far East. Its 269 crew and passengers were killed. Accusation and counter-accusation flew: it was hard to be certain what the Soviet pilots had and hadn't known about KAL007 or what warnings had been given or received. Even so, Reagan's characterization of the attack as a 'massacre' didn't seem so far off the mark.

A NEW BROOM

The suggestion that the USSR was a 'gerontocracy' has to be made with a degree of caution. Ronald Reagan had been a few days shy of 70 when he came to office for the first time. That said, this did make him the oldest first-term president the United States had yet seen. In the Soviet Union, it seemed more or less an average age. Sixty-eight when he succeeded the 75-year-old Leonid Brezhnev, Yuri Andropov died just two years later, in 1984. His successor, Konstantin Chernenko, was hardly in good health when he was appointed premier at the age of 70 and lasted only a little over a year.

Full 20 years his junior, Mikhail Gorbachev became premier in March 1985, when he was only in his mid-50s. He belonged to a completely different generation and it showed – not just in his physical vigour, but also in a friendly, informal personal style that many people saw reflected in the glamorous charisma of his wife, Raisa.

It was also evident in an ideological flexibility and an openness to new ideas that simply wouldn't have been available to any of his predecessors. They hadn't just been products of the Communist Party (Gorbachev had been that, too); they had been formed by the history they had lived through. Namely, the Stalin era – a time when ruthless discipline, secrecy and paranoia had reigned at home and the USSR had presented a hostile, defensive face to the outside world.

A CO-OPERATIVE SPIRIT
A guest in Reagan's White House, Mikhail Gorbachev sits down with his host to sign the Intermediate-Range Nuclear Forces Treaty (INF), 1987. To evade the restrictions placed on ICBMs by SALT II, it was alleged, the USSR had developed shorter-range weapons that placed Europe in the line of nuclear fire.

OUT OF AFGHANISTAN
An armoured column crosses the bridge at Termez, on the Afghan–Soviet border, its soldiers clearly relieved to be coming home. A seemingly endless drain on the USSR – militarily, economically, socially (and maybe morally as well) – the war had failed to fulfil any of its stated aims.

ПО ПЪТЯ на УНГАРИЯ
КЪДЕ СИ ТИ ЛЮБОВ НАРОДНА
Т. ЖИВКОВ САМ ЛИ ИЗВЪРШИ ТЕЗИ БЕЗ

Seen by the West in relatively general, depersonalized terms as a global conflict, World War II had been experienced by the Soviets as a fight for survival: a 'Great Patriotic War'. There were good reasons why the generation who had fought might have come to confuse rigidity with rightness and obduracy with integrity, but they weren't reasons that made sense in the modern age.

Soviet Communism had brought a backward country into the 20th century; it had industrialized an agrarian economy. It could also be seen as having led the fight against fascism in the war: it had arguably come to the rescue of the West. In addition, it had achieved great things in science and technology. And yet, for the most part, its citizens lived in permanent austerity; safe from real want but condemned by the system to mean and spartan lives.

Gorbachev pointed out the paradox. 'Our rockets can find Halley's comet …' he would say: 'but many household appliances are of poor quality.' Workers in the West might be oppressed, their 'surplus value' siphoned off by evil employers, but they had TVs, Hi-Fis, fridges and cars that worked. Thanks to the trade unionism the capitalist economies had (however grudgingly) accepted, they had pay and benefits of which their Soviet comrades could only dream. And they had access to a rich and colourful consumer culture – everything from foreign holidays to films and fashion. To the Old Communists, such enthusiasms might seem shallow. To the younger generation, though, these things mattered.

DESPERATE MEASURES

But the USSR was struggling even to maintain its defences year by year. Any aspiration beyond that seemed impossibly ambitious. Gorbachev accordingly proposed a policy of perestroika – a wholesale 'restructuring' of the economic system. To allow such radical change, a transformation in Soviet politics was going to be needed; this would in turn require a wholesale shift in attitudes.

He described the new outlook he was seeking as glasnost, or 'openness' – though what it actually amounted to was greater freedom – of speech, publication and political activism but also of entrepreneurship and investment. Of diplomacy, too: Gorbachev made high-profile visits to the West. (He was, Britain's Conservative Prime Minister Mrs Margaret Thatcher was famously to find, 'a man one could do business with'.)

These changes were almost unimaginably drastic, Gorbachev admitted – but, he maintained, absolutely essential if a chronically crisis-ridden Soviet Union was to be saved. Meanwhile, in hopes of bringing defence spending under some kind of control, he would work hard with the West to increase arms control. One of his first actions on ascending to power had been to announce a moratorium in nuclear testing that he had then extended a year later. The accession of Mohammad Najibullah's National Reconciliation government in 1987 allowed him to order a withdrawal from Afghanistan from May 1988.

OPPOSITE ABOVE:
BUSINESS PARTNER
British Prime Minister Margaret Thatcher meets President Mikhail Gorbachev at RAF base Brize Norton, December 1987. Margaret Thatcher is said to have remarked: 'I like Mr Gorbachev. We can do business together.'

OPPOSITE BELOW:
PEOPLE POWER
Give the people an inch, previous communist leaders had known, and they would take a democratic mile. Gorbachev's glasnost policy had always come with major risks. By 1989, unrest was growing across the Iron Curtain countries. Here, in Sofia, Bulgaria, vast crowds turned out to demand free elections. This sort of thing had ended badly before in Budapest and Prague. But Gorbachev's (December 1988) undertaking that the USSR would not intervene in its allies' internal affairs had emboldened the people in their calls for freedom.

LIGHTS IN THE DARKNESS
Czechoslovakians light candles in honour of protesters injured by police at the outset of the so-called 'Velvet Revolution'. The violent suppression of a student demonstration in Prague, on 17 November 1989, had only brought further protesters on to the streets in their tens of thousands. In the days that followed, the action had snowballed and spread across Czechoslovakia as a whole. The country's communist rulers had no idea what to do – and now no prospect of being rescued by their Soviet sponsors. On 28 November, the Party surrendered power.

HOMEWARD BOUND
Soviet forces start pulling out of Hungary, 25 April 1989. The Central Committee of the Hungarian Communist Party had already acknowledged that it would have to relinquish power. Round-table talks were therefore under way between a range of democratic parties about the best way forward for the country. The first free elections would be held just over a year later.

DRAWING THE CURTAIN

The settlement agreed at Yalta was rapidly unravelling.
In April 1989, the Polish government recognized
Solidarnosc. By the end of the month, Soviet forces were
pulling out of Hungary. In East Germany, a 'Peaceful
Revolution' was under way. By September, refugees
were streaming out to Austria through Czechoslavakia
and Poland. Their governments were still nominally
communist, but struggling to hold the line.

The Berlin Wall fell on 9 November 1989, a moment
as iconic as its construction had been – but much more
upbeat. The national border between the GDR and the
Federal Republic followed, allowing East Germans to
make their way directly west. On 3 December, the East
German government threw in the towel.

By this time Bulgaria's ruling Communist Party
had already been ousted; just over a fortnight later,
Czechoslovakia followed suit. Romania got the perfect
Christmas present with the overthrow of Nicolae
Ceauşescu on 25 December. The decade ended with
Václav Havel becoming the first democratically elected
president of Czechoslovakia, on 29 December.

ABOVE & OPPOSITE:
BREAKING OUT

The Berlin Wall had in its grungy, grey, concrete
blankness emblematized the ugliness of Germany's
ideological divisions, despite the best efforts of the
graffiti artists. The attack on it combined elements of
festivity and frenzy as Berliners vented the pent-up
frustration of decades. East German border guards
looked on impassively (above) as the protesters set
to work. Soon, the Wall was being systematically
destroyed (opposite).

OVERLEAF:
LOOKING FORWARD

Berliners enjoy the view from atop the barrier that had
divided their city for over three decades. For much of
its length, the wall was topped with anti-climb coping.
This had been omitted near the touristic Brandenburg
Gate, making this the perfect place to relax and breathe
the air of freedom.

DAVID 89
TWA
MAR
SUZANNE

ABOVE & RIGHT:
REVOLUTION IN ROMANIA
Soldiers and civilians made
common cause in the uprising
against Romania's ruler,
Nicolae Ceauşescu. Here
(left), they hide behind a
tank, taking cover from
heavy fire from the dictator's
loyal Securitate secret police,
while (right) a protester
waves a Romanian flag, the
Communist Party insignia at
its centre removed.

OPPOSITE:
COMMON CAUSE
Practical politics can be
a grubby game. Western
leaders were naturally eager
to associate themselves with
the idealism of the freedom
movement in the Eastern
Bloc; democracy campaigners
there understandably valued
their support. Here, US
President George H.W. Bush
(right) joins Lech Walesa at a
Solidarity rally in Poland.

SOLIDARNOŚĆ
WITA PREZYDENTA BUSH'A
SOLIDARNOŚĆ
PRACY

RIGHT:

FERVENT FOR REFORM

Since Mao's death, Deng Xiaoping had been trying to open up the economy without at the same time weakening the Party's political hold on China. As Mikhail Gorbachev had found, this was a challenge. Tiananmen Square was Beijing's principal public space. In 1966, at the start of the Cultural Revolution, a million young Red Guards had assembled to swear their life-and-death loyalty to Chairman Mao. Now, in April 1989, several thousand young democracy campaigners set up camp here to put pressure on the Communist Party to make reforms. Some 300,000 people had joined the Tiananmen protest at its height, around the end of May; there were similar protests in hundreds of other Chinese cities.

OVERLEAF:

QUIET COURAGE

Deng Xiaoping was disconcerted by the scale and passion of the pro-democracy protests. His comrades in the Party leadership were deeply unimpressed. Ordering that the demonstrators disperse, they threatened violent action but, though many left, over 100,000 still remained.

On 3 June 1989, soldiers sent into the square with tanks opened up with automatic weapons. Over the following few days, while passive resistance to their advance continued, the PLA continued to clear the square and its surrounding streets. Sometimes they contented themselves with kicking and beating the demonstrators but in many cases they also resumed shooting. By the time the crisis was over, several thousand protestors had been killed.

The sight of the lone protester standing in confrontation with a line of advancing tanks became iconic and is now known around the world.

1990s

January 1990 saw the opening of Moscow's first McDonald's in Pushkinskaya Square. Customers queued for hours for a taste of Western style. And of capitalist efficiency: the sight of a system working like clockwork was a frisson in itself for those accustomed to the organized chaos of a Soviet Union in which delays and shortages were the norm. And the citizens simply had to suck it up. Westerners might wince at the fatuous faux-friendliness of their service staff but it beat the impression socialist enterprises invariably gave that the customer was there on sufferance and should be grateful for whatever the state deigned to provide. Now, they marvelled to see their orders fulfilled to their exact specifications in a matter of mere seconds; to eat their meals at clean, bright tables in relaxed, convivial surroundings.

Pushkinskaya Square had been named in honour of the great Russian Romantic poet Alexander Pushkin. His impressive statue had been the main landmark here but now it had a rival in the Golden Arches sign.

UNDER NEW MANAGEMENT
Just sworn in as president of the Russian Republic, Boris Yeltsin (centre) exudes businesslike purpose. Like Gorbachev, a graduate of the school of Communist Party thinking, Yeltsin was yet more radical in his reformist views. Where his predecessor had contemplated change to save what he saw as the communist achievement, Yeltsin sought a wholesale switch to free-market economics and democratic pluralism.

A sign was all it was, of course. The new restaurant couldn't communicate its streamlined efficiency to a Soviet economy still mired in restrictive practices or its ethos of service to what had always been a bureaucratic tyranny. If the Moscow McDonald's mattered, it was as an emblem of those Western values the people now aspired to and their government felt ready – at least cautiously – to entertain.

BREAKING FREE

'You can't make an omelette without breaking eggs,' Stalin had supposedly said. Unmaking the omelette had proven no less difficult or damaging. Just as the hardline communist critics had warned, glasnost (p. 191) had opened up the USSR to a play of political differences, regional rivalries and local patriotisms that could hardly help but be centrifugal in its effects.

Mikhail Gorbachev's USSR had by now already lost a good deal of its East European empire (p. 197). Meanwhile, the stresses were showing in the Baltic states (Estonia, Latvia, Lithuania), in the Caucasus (Georgia, Armenia, Azerbaijan …), the western republics (Belarus and Moldova) and in Central Asia (Kazakhstan, Turkmenistan, Tajikistan …). Strong and insistent separatist movements had sprung up in all these republics: the Soviet Union was hardly a union at all.

RIGHT:
CORPSE OF COMMUNISM
It had been on Christmas Day 1989 that the Romanian dictator Nicolae Ceaușescu had been executed. Now, in March 1990, the first pictures were officially released. Clearly sickening for some time now, communism was apparently all but dead in Eastern Europe. How long could it last in the USSR?

OVERLEAF:
RED REACTION
The 'August Coup' wasn't just serious: it upended what had come to seem the natural communist order. It might have been déjà vu for Budapest and Prague, but seeing Soviet tanks deployed on city streets was for Moscow a deeply shocking and depressing first.

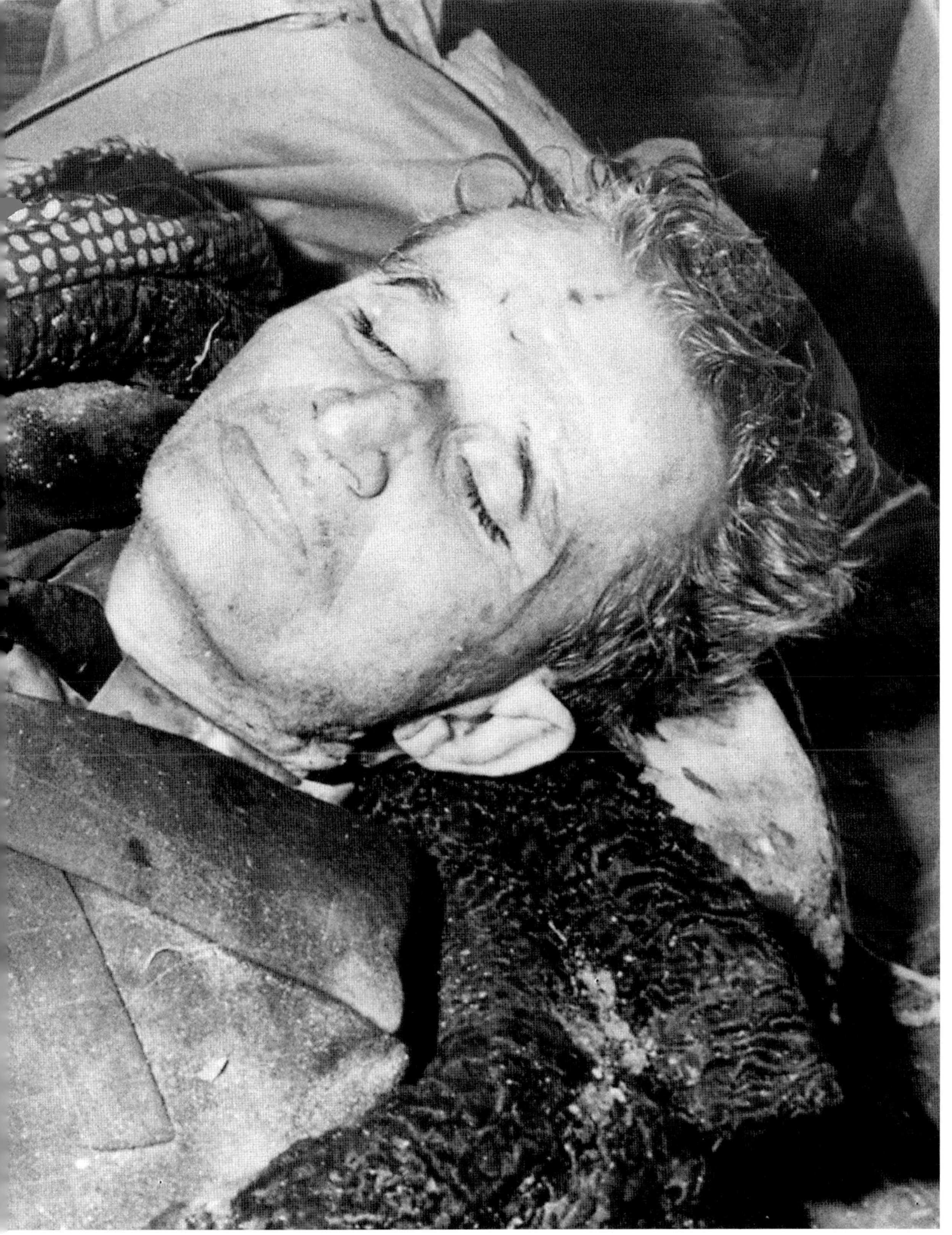

МОЛОКО
120

2
126

CHALLENGING THE COUP

The 'August Coup' of 1991 threatened to throw the whole reform process into reverse. Thousands of ordinary Muscovites turned out to protest. It was difficult to dispute the conspirators' claims that Gorbachev's policies had jeopardized Soviet integrity and prestige, given the desperate economic situation and the crumbling away of the union around its edges. However, many felt passionately that the price was worth paying, a life of freedom and opportunity far preferable to one of loyal subjection to an essentially authoritarian regime.

LEFT:

FREEDOM!

On 9 April 1991, following a referendum a few weeks before, the Republic of Georgia declared its independence from the USSR. Here, amidst scenes of general jubilation on the streets of Tbilisi, a young patriot registers his defiance. The Soviet Union had from the first encompassed a bewildering array of different nationalities and cultures. Maintaining a single overarching order had taken all the authoritarianism of communist ideology – and, of course, the ever-present threat of force.

If anything did unite these states it was a public mood poised delicately between liberationist exhilaration and economic dread. A slowly stagnating Soviet economy had at least assured its citizens some minimal measure of security. Now, the economy nosedived as the country descended into chaos. As 1990 gave way to 1991, these divisions only deepened.

RED REACTION

The disintegration of the USSR shocked everybody, in both East and West. It caused the deepest consternation in the country. Especially, of course, among the Communist Party old guard. Many felt that Mikhail Gorbachev had gone beyond boldness and tipped into reckless irresponsibility.

In August 1991, a group of diehards in government and the military made a coup attempt, sending troops to surround the Russian parliament building, the 'White House'. Soviet democracy, in so far as it existed, was taken hostage; Mikhail Gorbachev was taken prisoner, arrested at his dacha (country holiday home). His refusal to buckle disconcerted the rebels.

Meanwhile, anti-communist feeling was successfully mobilized by Gorbachev's longstanding critic, Boris Yeltsin. Like the premier, he had impressive communist credentials but had come to believe that free-market reforms and political democratization were needed. He didn't feel that Gorbachev's reforms had been anything like sweeping enough.

RIGHT:
BOWING OUT
Soviet premier Mikhail Gorbachev reads out his resignation statement. On the face of it, his career had ended in failure and many in Russia still see it that way, but in the wider world he's generally regarded as a historic figure.

ASSERTING INDEPENDENCE
The Supreme Soviet of the Ukrainian Soviet Socialist Republic had declared its independence from the USSR in August 1991. It asked the electorate to approve its decision in a referendum that December. Support was overwhelming. Here, at one of a series of pre-referendum rallies, an enthusiastic crowd waves Ukrainian flags.

Yeltsin had won sufficient support in Russia to be elected the Republic's president that year but had struggled to assert himself against a Gorbachev-dominated party.

Now, however, he came to his leader's rescue – though the Party secretary would have to pay a price in the form of influence ceded to Yeltsin, his country's coming man. Gorbachev was to find himself increasingly marginalized in the months that followed as first the Communist Party of the Soviet Union then the Soviet Union itself collapsed. With the replacement of the USSR by an already rather creaky 'Commonwealth of Independent States' (CIS) that December, Gorbachev no longer had a real role. In the years that followed, Yeltsin's remodelling of Russia would succeed in some ways but only at staggering cost, entrenching enormous inequalities and structural corruption.

'A NEW WORLD ORDER'

Without a USSR there could be no Cold War. To put it at its very crudest, the West had won. As far as the West had been concerned, China had always been secondary to the Soviet Union as a Cold War antagonist. Not because it lacked importance but because, historically introverted, it had played a much less active geopolitical role till now. Besides, whatever shortcomings it might have with regard to human rights, China had since the death of Chairman Mao been building a 'socialist market economy' that was much more acceptable to the capitalist countries of the West.

The United States had already claimed its prize. Speaking in Aspen, Colorado in August 1990, President George H.W. Bush had spoken of a 'New World Order' in which his country remained sole superpower. There was, he announced, to be a 25 per cent cut in US defence spending. A new spirit was abroad. Western leaders tried hard not to sound triumphalist, focusing instead on the new opportunities that had been opened up for all by this 'peace dividend'.

The sunlit uplands quickly clouded over. Bush's Secretary of State Colin Powell put it well when he lamented the fact that 'We no longer have the luxury of a threat to plan for'. A cynic might say – and many did – that such views represented the attempts of the military-industrial complex to come up with a new justification for their existence. But the next few decades would bring an array of foreign policy challenges, from international narco-trafficking through Islamic radicalism; from a newly expansionist Russia to climate change.

AS GOOD AS IT GETS
Watched by George H.W. Bush, Boris Yeltsin speaks to the press in the Rose Garden of the White House. The two presidents had agreed an important deal on arms reductions. Yeltsin could be charismatic but his style of government became increasingly erratic as time went by. He had always been a maverick, but his slide into alcoholism can't have helped.

MEMORY WALL
Visitors place flowers at the Berlin Wall Memorial in Berlin on 9 November 2018, during commemorations to mark the anniversary of the fall of the Berlin Wall. The fall of the Wall in a bloodless revolution on 9 November 1989 ended 28 years of Cold War separation.

Picture Credits

Alamy: 14 top (Fremantle), 21 top (Interfoto), 21 bottom (Everett Collection Historical), 26 & 30 top (World History Archive), 40 (Granger Historical Picture Archive), 42 bottom (IanDagnall Computing), 67 bottom (Interfoto), 92/93 (dpa picture alliance), 94/95 (IanDagnall Computing), 96 (Glasshouse Images), 97 (Everett Collection Historical), 100 top (CPA Media), 120/121 (US Marines Photo), 122/123 (Keystone Press), 124/125 (Reuters), 132/133 (Interfoto), 142/143 (Science History Images), 148/149 (Granger Historical Picture Archive), 196 (Pictorial Press), 198/199 (imageBROKER)

Getty Images: 5 (Popperfoto), 6 bottom (Mirrorpix), 14 bottom (AFP), 16/17 (Pictures From History/ Universal Images Group), 22/23 (AFP), 24/25 (Universal Images Group), 30 bottom (Archive Photos), 35 (Haywood Magee/Picture Post), 36/37 (Roger Viollet), 39 (Universal Images Group), 53 (Keystone), 54/55 (Popperfoto), 56/57 (Pictures from History), 58 (Popperfoto), 62 bottom (Fox Photos), 63 (Corbis), 66 (Universal Images Group), 67 top (Keystone), 72/73 (Popperfoto), 76 (SovFoto), 78 (Keystone-France), 79 (AFP), 80 & 81 (Keystone-France), 82 (Michael Ochs Archives), 84 top (Universal Images Group), 86/87, 90/91 & 98 (Keystone), 104/105 (J. Wilds), 110 top (Tim Page), 110 bottom (SovFoto), 111 (Bride Lane Library/ Popperfoto), 112/113 (Keystone), 113 (The Asahi Shimbun), 114/115 (Vittoriano Rastelli), 116/117 (Rolls Press/ Popperfoto), 126/127 (SovFoto), 128 (Pictures from History), 138/139 (Henri Bureau), 144 (Horacio Villalobos), 146/147 (Julio Donoso), 150/151 (Consolidated News Pictures), 152 (Jacques Pavlovsky), 153 (Roland Neveu), 156 (AFP), 157 bottom (Roland Neveu), 160/161 (Kurita Kaku), 162 & 163 (Penny Tweedie), 165 (Keystone), 168 (Manoukian Pascal), 169 top (Alain Mingam), 169 bottom (Archive Photos), 170/171 (Chuck Fishman), 172 (Corbis), 174/175 (Sygma), 177 (Wojtek Laski), 178/179 (Bride Lane Library/Popperfoto), 180/181 (Dick Halstead), 182/183 (Bob Thomas), 184/185 (Miroslav Zajic), 187 (Dick Halstead), 188/189 (AFP), 190 top (Mirrorpix), 190 bottom (Joel Robine/AFP), 192/193 (Peter Turnley), 194/195 (Eric Bouvet/Gamma-Rapho), 197 (Colin C. Campbell), 200 both (Peter Turnley), 201 (Diana Walker), 202/203 (Peter Charlesworth), 204/205 (Archive Photos), 206 (Sergei Guneyev), 208/209 (AFP), 210/211 & 212/213 (Alain Nogues/Sygma), 214/215 (Andrei Gorelowsky/AFP), 216/217 (Vitaly Armand/AFP), 218/219 (Anatoly Sapronenkov/AFP), 221 (Ron Sachs/Consolidated News Photos), 222/233 (Ralf Hirschberger/DPA/AFP)

Getty Images/Bettmann Archive: 28/29, 31, 33, 38, 42 top, 43 both, 44/45, 60/61, 62 top, 64/65, 69, 70, 71 both, 84 bottom, 88/89, 99, 100 bottom, 103, 108/109, 118/119, 130 both, 134/135, 136/137, 140/141, 154/155, 157 top, 158/159, 164, 166/167

Licensed under the Creative Commons Attribution-Share Alike 3.0 Unported License: 74/75 (Fortepan)

Licensed under the GNU Free Documentation License: 7 (San Jose)

iStock: 6 top (btgbtg)

Library of Congress: 8

National Archives and Records Administration: 10, 11 both, 32, 46/47, 48, 50/51, 101, 107

Public Domain: 12/13

U.S. Department of Defense: 18/19